Places to Go
with Children
IN THE
DELAWARE VALLEY

Places to Go with Children

IN THE
DELAWARE VALLEY

Alice Rowan O'Brien

Chronicle Books ▪ *San Francisco*

Printed in the United States of America.

Library of Congress Cataloging in Publication Data
O'Brien, Alice Rowan.
  Places to go with children in the Delaware Valley.

  Includes index.
  1. Delaware River Valley (Penn.-Del. and N.J.)—Description and travel—Guide-books.
  2. Family recreation—Delaware River Valley (Penn.-Del. and N.J.)—Guide-books.   I. Title.
F157.D4037   1989   917.49′0443   88-37689
ISBN 0-87701-581-3

Editing: Carolyn Miller
Book and cover design: Seventeenth Street Studios
Composition: Another Point, Inc.

10 9 8 7 6 5 4 3 2 1

Chronicle Books
275 Fifth Street
San Francisco, California
94103

Contents

Introduction

It was the third rainy, raw Saturday morning in February. Once again, my three-year-old son was glued to the TV, hypnotized by the antics and inter-actions of the Smurfs. I bear no prejudice toward these small blue elves who speak in a peculiar manner. The mind control they exercise over kid-dos is relatively harmless. It just depressed me to think that yet another precious weekend, albeit a rainy one, had gotten off to such an uninspired, unproductive start. Determined to find a suitable daytime activity that would get our small family out and about, I searched for the weekend en-tertainment section of the Friday evening newspaper. My quest ended in the trash can. Upon this treasure trove of information had been heaped the scraps of the previous night's salmon dinner.

It was at that moment that the idea for writing *Places to Go with Children in the Delaware Valley* occurred to me—I decided to create a permanent reference work listing "child-friendly" attractions such as museums, his-toric sites, special parks, and zoos.

As a child growing up in rural Lancaster County, Pennsylvania, I have fond summer memories of picking fresh fruits and veggies one day and taking part in a family project of converting them to jams, jellies, or freezer fillers the next. In Lancaster, having a Christmas tree you didn't choose from a field and chop down yourself was unheard of. Farms where you can "pick your own" were therefore added to what was then an imaginary outline.

Thanks to Chronicle Books editor Nion T. McEvoy and many helpful people at area attractions, chambers of commerce, and visitors' bureaus, the idea became a reality. I hope that children who reside in or visit the re-gion, their parents, doting aunts and uncles, teachers and child-care givers will enjoy using the book as much as I have enjoyed writing it.

Organized by state and county, the book covers attractions in the Dela-ware Valley's most populous area: mid- to northern Delaware, south to central New Jersey, and the five Pennsylvania counties that include and sur-round Greater Philadelphia. The places selected for inclusion in the book are permanent attractions with either year-round or set seasonal hours. Many more attractions exist than are listed in the book; the emphasis here is on places where children and the adults who accompany them can have a pleasant time together. As a help to teachers, camp directors, and day-care administrators, information on special children's groups services of-fered by many of the attractions has been included. Annual Delaware Valley special events are listed month by month in the back of the book. Because

schedules and admissions fees are subject to change, call your chosen destination ahead of time for up-to-the-minute information.

Please let us know about special Delaware Valley places that you and
your children discover, along with your opinions of or comments on those
listed in the book. Until then, put the Smurfs on hold and enjoy a family
outing to one of the region's rich array of entertaining and educational
places.

Delaware

Known as the Diamond State and the Blue Hen State, and as "Small Wonder" by the Delaware Tourism Office, Delaware's most notable achievement was becoming "the state that started a nation." In 1787, Delaware, by being the first former colony to ratify the U.S. Constitution, became the first state of the fledgling United States. Permanent Swedish and Dutch settlements were established in Delaware in the early and mid-16th century, predating the ratification of the U.S. Constitution by nearly a century and a half.

Another Delaware history highlight was the arrival of E.I. du Pont de Nemours from France in 1801. On the banks of the Brandywine River in northern Delaware's New Castle County, du Pont and his young family established a gunpowder manufactory and milling community, the predecessor of what is now one of the world's largest chemical companies. Many of Delaware's major cultural attractions were conceived and established by du Pont family members as the business grew and prospered in the early 20th century. Delaware's pro-business attitude has made it an attractive home for other chemical companies and, more recently, a banking and insurance industry. Statewide charitable and cultural organizations are enriched by the financial and moral support Delaware businesses and industries lend.

Delaware may be short on size but it's long on character, with an identity, a history, and a culture that are related to but separate from its larger Delaware Valley neighbors, Pennsylvania and New Jersey. Come and discover some of the places that make the Small Wonder one of the best stops in the region.

A roll mill demonstration at Hagley Museum

New Castle County

City of Wilmington

Brandywine Zoo

1001 North Park Drive, Wilmington, DE. (302) 571-7788. Daily, 10 a.m. to 4 p.m. April through October: Children 3 to 12, 75¢; adults, $2. Free November through March.

The Brandywine Zoo, located in Brandywine Park across Park Drive from the riverbank, is an easy family destination, especially for parents with infants and toddlers. While its exhibits may not be as numerous or elaborate as those in bigger city zoos, the zoo's limited scope is also its charm. Little ones enjoy the animal panorama without being overwhelmed. The zoo is home to an assortment of four-footed creatures including llamas, raccoons, bobcats, black bears, tigers, foxes, otters, and capybaras. Owls, macaws, and assorted native birds and waterfowl are also on view. If the kiddos want an up-close and personal animal encounter, a hands-on visit with the miniature goats in the self-service petting zoo will do the trick.

Snacks, drinks, and ice cream treats are available in the zoo's commissary from May to October. Pack a picnic lunch to eat on the riverbank rocks across the street before or after your visit.

African Waterhole Exhibit, Delaware Museum of Natural History

Fort Christina
*Foot of Seventh Street, Wilmington, DE. (302) 652-5629. Daily, 8 a.m. to
sunset. Free.*

Site of the Swedish landing in 1638 and the first permanent settlement in
the Delaware Valley, this state-owned park was recently spiffed up for the
celebration of the 350th anniversary of the Swedes' arrival. A monument
created by sculptor Carl Milles and given by the people of Sweden to the
people of Delaware on the 300th anniversary, portrays the Swedes landing
in their pioneer flagship, the *Kalmar Nyckle.* A rustic log cabin stands near
the memorial, a reminder that the Swedes were the first in America to use
this building technique.

Delaware Art Museum
*2301 Kentmere Parkway, Wilmington, DE. (302) 571-9590. Tuesday,
10 a.m. to 9 p.m.; Wednesday through Saturday, 10 a.m. to 5 p.m.; Sunday,
noon to 5 p.m. Free; donation encouraged.*

This regional museum of fine arts recently expanded its galleries to showcase its permanent collections of American paintings and illustrations from
1840 to the present and English Pre-Raphaelite works from the Victorian
age. Changing exhibits include temporary shows traveling from art centers
across the country and special exhibitions of photographs, contemporary
crafts, sculpture, prints, and posters drawn from the museum's collection.
    Particularly pleasing to the bambinos are the works of Howard Pyle,
known as the father of American illustration and the founder of the Brandywine school of painting. His painted pirate scenes and visual interpreta-
tions of the King Arthur legends have sparked the imaginations of
generations of children and continue to cast the same pleasant spell.
    The museum's participatory gallery is a "must do" with children. The
current installation, "Pegafoamasaurus," is scheduled through 1990. Kids
enter one room in which doors of varying sizes, painted in primary colors,
are used as vehicles to explain the elements of art: shape, line, color, tex-
ture, and space. Through one of the doors, they enter the second gallery
room. There they find three walls of white pegs. In the room's center are
bins of brightly colored foam shapes with peg-sized holes cut in the center
of each. Armed with their new-found knowledge of the elements of art and
their own creative instincts, kids can happily and safely create their own
works as they establish and improve their visual literacy. After 1990, another interactive, child-pleasing installation is scheduled. A stop in the mu-

seum store is warranted. There's a special section devoted to kids' toys, books, and gadgets. The museum is adjacent to Rockford Park, an ideal place for a family picnic.

Old Swedes' Church and Hendrikson House Museum
606 Church Street, Wilmington, DE. (302) 652-5629. Tuesday through Saturday, noon to 4 p.m. 50¢ per person.

One of the oldest churches in the United States, standing as originally built and regularly used for religious services, Old Swedes' Church was built in 1698. The Hendrikson House Museum, a two-room Swedish farmhouse next to the church, was constructed in 1690. One room is a restored farm kitchen with implements, tools, and furnishings of the period. The second room features a display of documents and artifacts from the church's archives. While no special children's tours or activities are sponsored, museum guides make an effort to interact with and give special attention to youngsters touring the facility with their parents.

Old Town Hall
505 Market Street Mall, Wilmington, DE. (302) 655-7161. Tuesday through Friday, noon to 4 p.m.; Saturday, 10 a.m. to 4 p.m. Free.

Built in 1798, Old Town Hall was restored to its original appearance by the Historical Society of Delaware, which is headquartered there. On the first floor, young visitors can view the society's changing exhibits along with its permanently displayed nine-foot-tall wooden statue of George Washington and Revolutionary and Civil War flags. Upstairs, paintings of famous Delawareans are presented along with collections of early silver and furniture made in the state. The second floor also features a children's room with a toy collection and a large and elaborately furnished dollhouse. The five-foot-high dollhouse was won by a Wilmington man during a raffle held in Philadelphia to support the care of injured soldiers during the Civil War. Across the mall in Willingtown Square, an enclave of six 18th-century houses restored by the society, is a gift shop, the Eclectic Depot. It stocks a nice selection of inexpensive games, toys, and souvenirs for kids.

Kids peer at an antique dollhouse in Old Town Hall.

Port of Wilmington
Christina and Terminal avenues, Wilmington, DE. (302) 571-4600. Monday through Friday, 8 a.m. to 4 p.m. Free tours by appointment.

Kids love the sights and sounds of the recently improved and enlarged Port of Wilmington, the closest Delaware River port to the open Atlantic Ocean. They see the entire operation: ocean-going vessels being docked and giant 100-ton cranes loading and off-loading exported and imported products. It's worth making the effort to call ahead.

United States Coast Guard Cutter *Mohawk*
Foot of King Street and the Christina River. (302) 656-0400. Saturday, 9 a.m. to 3 p.m. or by appointment. Free.

Constructed by Wilmington ship builders from the Pusey & Jones Company in 1934, the *Mohawk* now serves as a museum and memorial to the Coast Guard, Navy, and Merchant Marine seamen who served aboard her during the World War II battle for the North Atlantic. Originally constructed to serve as a domestic ice breaker and rescue vessel, the *Mohawk* performed many additional duties when the United States entered the war. Visitors can walk her decks and tour her restored staterooms and berths. World War II memorabilia relating to the ship and her crew is also on display.

Brandywine Valley

Brandywine Creek State Park
Adams Dam Road (intersection of Routes 100 and 92), Wilmington, DE. (302) 571-3534 or 655-5740. Daily, 8 a.m. to sunset. Memorial Day to Labor Day: Cars with Delaware tags, $2 for the first two passengers, 50¢ for each additional passenger; cars with out-of-state tags, $4 for the first two passengers, 50¢ for each additional passenger.

A regional park set in the dramatic hills and valleys along the Brandywine, Brandywine Creek State Park is a special place for children in all seasons. When the first good snow hits the ground, it's the place in northern Delaware for sledding and cross-country skiing. The hiking trails through its woodlands, fields, thickets, and marshlands are a pleasure any time. Fishing is also permitted. Outdoor picnicking facilities and a pavilion are available, as are restrooms. Special seasonal reserved family and children's programs are scheduled throughout the year, including a campfire at Halloween and a nature scavenger hunt in the spring.

Delaware Museum of Natural History
Route 52, Greenville, DE. (302) 658-9111. Monday through Saturday, 9:30 a.m. to 4:30 p.m.; Sunday, noon to 5 p.m. Children, $1.75; adults, $2.50.

Find out who turns up for a drink at an African waterhole. Tiptoe over the Great Barrier Reef. See the world's largest bird egg or a 500-pound clam. Check out a seashell collection of over a million specimens. Watch the

*Visitor hugs a stuffed bear cub in the
"Please Touch" Room at the Delaware
Museum of Natural History.*

daily nature film. These are just some of the things to do and see at the Delaware Museum of Natural History. Budding Darwins and kids who just love the great outdoors will enjoy the museum's dioramas and displays. Of special interest to half-pints is the Discovery Room, where they can touch real stuffed animals and participate in supervised science games.

Plan to stop by the museum's gift shop. It carries an unusual assortment of kids' games, toys, and doodads that relate to museum collections.

Delaware Nature Society/Ashland Nature Center

Brackenville and Barley Mill roads, Hockessin, DE. (302) 239-2334. Monday through Friday, 8:30 a.m. to 4:30 p.m.; Saturday, 9 a.m. to 3 p.m. Children, 50¢; adults, $1.25.

Discover the greatness of outdoor Delaware on the self-guided, well-marked hiking trails at Ashland Nature Center, nestled amidst 600 acres of meadows, pine and hardwood forests, marshes, and flood plains. Four different nature walks include the sights, sounds, textures, and smells associated with a variety of the natural habitats common in the state. The self-guided, hands-on Discovery Room for children features animal puppets, an Indian hut, and natural-science games kids are sure to enjoy. An imaginative selection of workbooks, coloring books, games, toys, and gadgets are available for sale in the gift shop along with well-known field guides, bird feeders, and T-shirts. Outdoor tables are available for picnicking. Special children's services include reserved group programs on subjects such as Delaware animals, Indians, maple sugaring, pond and wildlife ecology, and farm life. The center can also accommodate children's daytime birthday parties and sleep-overs by reservation.

Hagley Museum

Route 141, Greenville, DE. (302) 658-2400. January through March: Weekends, 9:30 a.m. to 4:30 p.m.; weekdays, 1:30 to 4:30 p.m. April through December: Daily, 9:30 a.m. to 4:30 p.m. Children 6 to 14, $2.50; children under 6, free; adults, $6.

An indoor-outdoor museum of 19th-century industry and life, Hagley, located on 230 acres of hills and vales that parallel the Brandywine River, is the site of the Du Pont Company black powder manufactory and workers' community. Although the tour is two to 2½ hours long, kids withstand it well because it's done by jitney bus, an amusement in itself. Visitors are

A walk through the restored French gardens of Eleutherian Mills at the Hagley Museum

transported to and from the museum's two dozen restored mills and homes to view exhibits on the development of water, steam, and electric power. They also look back into the lives of the company's owners and work force as they tour their restored homes, workshops, and schoolhouse. The live demonstrations at the 1880 machine shop, roll mill, and water-wheel are real child pleasers, as are the 19th-century activities that take place in the worker's cottage and school. Parents will enjoy Eleutherian Mills, the du Pont family's original Georgian homestead, with its formal restored garden.

Food is available, as are picnic facilities. Special children's services include reserved school and camp group tours that focus on such subjects as 19th-century life, U.S. industrial history, and energy resources and power. In addition to a well-stocked museum gift shop, there is Frizzell's Store for children. It features an interesting array of gifts of educational value at reasonable prices.

Rockwood/The Shipley-Bringhurst-Hargraves Museum

610 Shipley Road, Wilmington, DE. (302) 571-7776. Tuesday through Saturday, 11 a.m. to 3 p.m. Children 5 to 16, $1; children under 5, free; adults, $3.

Woodlands encircle Rockwood, inspired by an English country house and built in 1851 by Joseph Shipley, a Quaker merchant. Passed down through generations of the same family, this rural Gothic estate is now administered by New Castle County. It contains archives, furnishings, and decorative arts from the 17th to the early 20th century, including American, European, and Oriental objects. The grounds and gardens are a showcase of the Victorian romantic landscape style, emphasizing the unity of architecture with nature. Outdoor picnic facilities are available.

Special children's services include reserved school or camp group programs for a variety of age groups. Three different children's group programs are offered. "Edward's Birthday Party" is a look at how a child who lived in the house celebrated his big day around the turn of the century. "In Great-Grandmother's Time," a hands-on study of life 100 years ago, emphasizes genealogy. "Upstairs, Downstairs" is a program in which children play the roles of house servants to learn about Irish emigration and the interworkings of a Victorian household. "Gothic Gables and Fables," an unreserved children's day at the museum, is held annually on the first Saturday in October. That Saturday, all house tours are conducted from a child's perspective, and activities such as marionette shows and 19th-century story telling are scheduled.

Wilderness Canoe Trips

P.O. Box 7125, Wilmington, DE (behind Fairfax Shopping Center on Route 202). (302) 654-2227. Late May to mid-September. Fees vary based on trip length and number of passengers.

Interested in seeing the unspoiled landscape and elegant du Pont family country estates along the Brandywine from a unique perspective? The kids are sure to love the means of transportation offered by Wilderness Canoe Trips. The shallow waters of the Brandywine are the perfect place to enjoy a two- or four-hour canoe ride down the stream. Inner tubes are another rentable conveyance families use to travel the waterway on six- and two-hour trips. Call ahead to reserve your canoe or tube trip. The Wilderness people are happy to offer advice on trip lengths and equipment in relation to the age of the children in your party. Included in the reasonable fee is the equipment itself and your transportation to and from the launch and pick-up points along the river. Every member of the party is furnished with a regulation life jacket.

Wilmington & Western Railroad
Routes 41 and 2, Wilmington, DE. (302) 999-9008. Sunday, May through October. Trains depart at 12:30, 2, and 3:30 p.m. Children 2 to 12, $3; children under 2, free; adults, $5.

All aboard the Wilmington & Western Railroad, the state's only scenic tourist line. It's an experience that kids love and parents also enjoy. Every Sunday during its May through October operating season, the railroad runs three 1-hour round trips from Greenbank Station to the stream-side picnic grove at Mt. Cuba, Delaware's only mountain. From the windows of touring turn-of-the-century passenger cars, riders view the woodlands and open fields of the historic Red Clay Valley. The train's "baggage master" explains the history of the region and describes points of interest along the way.

Passengers board the train at the station complex, a Victorian structure that houses the ticket office, gift shop, and snack bar. Visitors waiting to board the train can browse the flea market adjacent to the station. Those who catch the first two Sunday trains can picnic at Mt. Cuba and ride a later train back to the station.

In addition to the seasonal schedule of Sunday trains, the railroad schedules family-oriented events throughout the year, including half-price admission days for kids, the Great American Train Robbery, the Halloween Ghost train, and the Santa Claus Special.

Special children's services include reserved Trains to History school and camp group tours and reserved rentals of the caboose on regular Sunday trips for birthday parties and other special occasions.

Winterthur Museum and Gardens
Route 52, Winterthur, DE. (302) 656-8591.
Tuesday through Saturday, 10 a.m. to 4 p.m.; Sunday, noon to 4 p.m. Children 12 to 16, $6.50; children under 12, free; adults, $8.

Winterthur provides its visitors with a unique opportunity to observe the physical surroundings of early American home life. Founded by Henry Francis du Pont, its world-famous collections of furniture, paintings, silver,

*Wilmington & Western Railroad's No. 98
rounds a trestle bridge.*

ceramics, glass, textiles, and prints are showcased in authentic period rooms, moved piece by piece from their original locations. While its orientation is definitely not toward little ones, older children would enjoy Winterthur's Two Centuries Tour, the museum's general open-admission tour that includes 15 rooms and covers the period 1640 to 1840. The museum's other more extensive subject and period tours are unavailable to those under 16 years of age and generally require advanced reservations. The admission fee to the 45-minute Two Centuries Tour also covers a tram ride through the estate's vast English country gardens. Winterthur's Pavilion Restaurant offers cafeteria-style and full-service lunchtime dining. Outdoor picnic facilities are also available. Winterthur's retail shops and galleries sell a vast selection of merchandise, from books, plants, and simple folk-art toys to high-style Chippendale furniture, reproduced from original pieces in the collection.

Special children's services include two reserved group programs. For kindergarten through grade six, it's the "Be a Detective" program. Students examine old utensils, tools, and clothing to discover clues about early American life. Seventh and eighth graders identify, measure, and discuss early objects and create their own exhibits in the "Be a Curator" program. Both programs include a tour of some of the museum's many rooms.

Town of New Castle

The town of New Castle was first known as Fort Casimir to the Dutch who founded the town in 1651 on their way up the Delaware River. Later conquered by the Swedes and then the British, it was the first landing site of William Penn in North America in 1682. New Castle appears to be "the town that time forgot," with its central green and cobblestone streets. The locals refer to New Castle as a preservation—versus a restoration—because many of its stately Georgian homes and public buildings have been maintained as they now appear for over two centuries. New Castle's colonial history, architecture, and picturesque waterfront make it an easy and comfortable place to enjoy with children. Pack the stroller and a picnic if you have little ones. Older kids would enjoy lunch at one of the town's quaint inns.

Amstel House Museum
Fourth and Delaware streets, New Castle, DE. (302) 322-2794 or 328-8215. April through November: Tuesday through Saturday, 11 a.m. to 4 p.m.; Sunday, 1 to 4 p.m. Children, 50¢; adults, $1.

The oldest section of this handsome home was built in 1680 by a Dutch settler and consisted of two rooms, one above the other. In 1730, the house was enlarged to its present appearance. Local legend has it that George Washington attended a wedding held here in 1784. The Amstel House is now furnished with decorative arts and artifacts of the period.

Battery Park
Delaware Street and the Delaware River. Free.

This little municipal park, located right on the riverbank, is the perfect place for a lunchtime stop or a breather from an afternoon of touring Old New Castle. Picnic tables and playground equipment are available.

George Read II House and Gardens
42 the Strand, New Castle, DE. (302) 322-8411. March through December: Tuesday through Saturday, 10 a.m. to 4 p.m.; Sunday, noon to 4 p.m. Children, $1; adults, $3.

Built between the years 1797 and 1804 on the banks of the Delaware, this elegant Federal mansion was owned by George Read II, a lawyer who signed the U.S. Constitution. His papa was the first George Read, a signer of the Declaration of Independence. The home's graceful exterior and interior carved woodwork, relief plasterwork, and gilded fanlights reflect the high Georgian style of its original owner. Its rooms provide a contrast between the Colonial Revivalist tastes of its last owner, who donated the property to the Historical Society of Delaware in 1975, and those of its earliest inhabitants. Don't miss the formal gardens that surround the house.

Immanuel Episcopal Church
The Green, New Castle, DE. (302) 328-2413. Daily, 10 a.m. to 4 p.m. Free.

Founded in 1689, this was the first Church of England parish in the state. The original structure was built in 1703 and burned to the ground in

1980, when cinders from a nearby marsh fire were blown onto the steeple. The church was lovingly rebuilt using the original foundations and walls, an exact replica in every detail of the building that had stood before. Visitors are welcome at all services.

Old Court House

Market and Delaware streets, New Castle, DE. (302) 323-4453. Tuesday through Saturday, 10 a.m. to 4:30 p.m.; Sunday, 1:30 to 4:30 p.m. Free.

Built in 1732, the Old Court House was Delaware's Colonial Capitol and the meetingplace of the State Assembly until 1777. Its spire is the compass point for Delaware's unusual circular northern border. Modified and remodeled throughout its history, the Old Court House now contains exhibits on Delaware history and government and serves as a visitors' information center for the town. Self-guided walking tour maps are available here. For that reason, the Old Court House makes a good first stop when you arrive in New Castle.

Old Dutch House Museum

32 East Third Street, New Castle, DE. (302) 322-9168 or 328-8215. April through November: Tuesday through Saturday, 11 a.m. to 4 p.m.; Sunday, 1 to 4 p.m. Children, 50¢; adults, $1.

This 1½-story abode predates some of the nearby 18th-century houses by well over 100 years. It's the last architectural relic of New Castle's period of 17th-century Dutch and Swedish settlements. Furnished with Colonial antiques, Old Dutch House, with its low ceilings, seems like a hostelry for elves. It confirms a well-known theory of anthropology: As a civilization ages and prospers, so grow its people.

Old Library Museum

40 East Third Street, New Castle, DE. (302) 328-8215. Thursday and Saturday, 11 a.m. to 4 p.m. Free.

This unusual hexagonal structure, built in 1892, is headquarters for the New Castle Historical Society. It houses exhibits on all aspects and periods of New Castle and Delaware history.

Old Presbyterian Church
25 East Second Sreet, New Castle, DE. (302) 328-3279. Daily, 10 a.m. to 4 p.m. Free.

Built in 1707, this church traces its ancestry to the Dutch settlers, some of whom are buried in unmarked graves in the adjacent cemetery. It was restored to its present appearance just after World War II. Visitors are welcome at all worship services.

Southern New Castle County

Fort Delaware
Foot of Clinton Street, Delaware City, DE. (302) 834-7941. May through September: Weekends and holidays, 11 a.m. to 6 p.m. Boat ride: Children under 15, $1.25; adults, $2.50.

Fort Delaware is a Civil War fortress located on Pea Patch Island, smack in the middle of the Delaware River. Built to defend the ports of Wilmington and Philadelphia to the north, the present fort was erected where two military fortifications had stood before: an earthworks with artillery built during the War of 1812, and a wooden fort begun in 1818 and later destroyed by fire in 1831. Construction of the present building was begun in 1848 and completed in 1859. From 1861 to 1865, it served as a Union prison for over 30,000 Confederate soldiers. Guided tours of the fort are conducted on the hour and announced by public address system or signs at the fort's entrance. Visitors may also tour by themselves. Admission to the fort is free, and includes a 30-minute narrated slide tape on the fort's history. There's a modest charge for the boat ride out.

Getting there is half the fun. Buy your boat tickets at the state-run dock at the foot of Clinton Street and hop aboard the *Miss Kathy,* an open-air touring boat, for a ten-minute ride through the Delaware River shipping channel out to the island. You'll be met by a tractor-drawn passenger cart and transported to the moat bridge at the fort's entrance. Pack a picnic. Outdoor tables and charcoal grills are available on the fort grounds. Beverages and candy can be purchased in the gift shop. If you have infants or toddlers, bring a backpack carrier. The fort's winding stairways and sky-high ramparts are shaky ground for a stroller.

A birdseye view of Fort Delaware

Historic Houses of Odessa

Main Street, Odessa, DE. (302) 378-4027. March though December, Tuesday through Saturday, 10 a.m. to 4:30 p.m.; Sunday, 1 to 4:30 p.m. Children under 12, free; adults, $6.

Winterthur Museum administers five historic properties that are located in this historic town whose citizens adopted the name Odessa in 1855, hoping that it would achieve status as a major grain port like the Ukraine's city of the same name. The Corbit-Sharp House is a handsome brick structure built in 1774 by local tanner William Corbit. Purchased, restored, furnished, and donated to Winterthur by its last owner, H. Rodney Sharp, the house was an integral part of the underground railroad. Kids are intrigued by its secret crawl space, used in the past for hiding runaway slaves seeking freedom in the north. Next door, the Wilson-Warner House is furnished to depict life along the river in the early 19th century. Other buildings include a stable and a shack for skinning muskrats, whose pelts and meat were part of the town's early economy. The 19th-century Brick Hotel houses a nationally famous collection of Victorian furniture.

When children take the standard tour of the Odessa properties with adults, the guides make every effort to involve them in the experience. Special family days are also part of the program. The annual Halloween, Christmas, and Spring Festival events are specifically geared to families. Special subject tours, tailor-made to fit the age and interest level of children's groups, can be arranged by reservation.

Iron Hill Museum

1355 Old Baltimore Pike, Newark, DE. (302) 368-5703. Wednesday through Friday, 11 a.m. to 4 p.m.; weekends, noon to 6 p.m. $1 per person, 5 and over; under 5, free.

This former schoolhouse is stuffed to the gills with a fascinating array of objects having to do with Delaware natural, social, and industrial history. There's a display on the state's early iron industry. Delaware wildlife is showcased in exhibits that include a stuffed elk, possums, birds, hawks, owls, and the immense shoulder blade of a whale. Fossils of Delaware fauna and flora are on view along with a collection of minerals, some of which are fluorescent. The life of the Lenni-Lenape Indians is interpreted inside in a diorama and outside in the recreated wigwam and sweat house. While the exhibits aren't exactly slick, kids learn a lot because the museum interpreters are trained to reach young audiences. Pack a picnic lunch to enjoy in the county park adjacent to the facility.

Special children's programs are a mainstay of the museum. There are reserved group tours, a week-long Indian Adventure summer camp, and archeology field programs conducted by the museum staff in the adjoining county park.

Lum's Pond State Park

Route 71, Kirkwood, DE. (302) 368-6989. Daily, 8 a.m. to sunset. Memorial Day to Labor Day: Cars with Delaware tags, $2 for the first two passengers, 50¢ for each additional passenger; cars with out-of-state tags, $4 for the first two passengers, 50¢ for each additional passenger.

If your kiddos like boating, this clean and well-kept park is worth a visit. Ride the waters of the 200-acre pond in one of the paddleboats, rowboats, canoes, or sunfish sailboats available for rental at the park dock. Don't forget the fishing gear. Lum's Pond sunnies and other small freshwater fish are waiting to bend a few rods. Enjoy a swim from the pond's beach and lunch at the snack bar or in one of the numerous picnic areas.

New Castle County "Pick Your Own" Farms

□ **Coleman's Tree Farm**
R.D. 2, P.O. Box 221, Middletown, DE 19707, (302) 378-2703.

Crops:	Christmas trees (Scotch pine, Douglas fir, Norway spruce).
Season, Hours:	Thanksgiving through Christmas Eve, daily from 8 a.m. to 5 p.m.
Directions:	Route 9, 1.5 miles east of Odessa, off Route 13.

□ **Greenspring Orchard**
Road 484, Smyrna, DE 19977, (302) 653-5142.

Crops:	Apples (Lodi, Early Blaze, Prima, Gala, and Red, Golden, and Blushing Golden Delicious).
Season, Hours:	July through November. Call ahead for hours.
Directions:	County Road 484 next to the railroad tracks.

□ **Marvin R. Hershberger Farm**
855 Canoe Club Road, Newark, DE 19702, (302) 738-5116.

Crops:	Strawberries.
Season, Hours:	Memorial Day to late June. Call ahead for hours.
Directions:	1.6 miles southwest of Christiana on the Old Baltimore Pike.

□ **Hickman's Christmas Tree Farm**
R.D. 2, P.O. Box 2347, Smyrna, DE 19977, (302) 653-6088.

Crops:	Christmas trees (white pine, and Norway, white and Serbia spruce).
Season, Hours:	Friday after Thanksgiving through December 23, 9 a.m. to 5 p.m.
Directions:	6 miles south of Odessa on Route 13 to Route 471 at Blackbird, to Road 470.

☐ La Villa Maria
R.D. 2, P.O. Box 2181, Smyrna, DE 19977, (302) 378-4576.

Crops:	Strawberries.
Season, Hours:	Mid-May to mid-June: Monday through Friday, 8 a.m. to 7 p.m.; Saturday and Sunday, 8 a.m. to 4 p.m.
Directions:	From Route 13, travel 6 miles south of Odessa and turn west on to County Road 471. Go 2.5 miles and look for the Spanish-style house with the tile roof.

☐ Lovett Farm
729 Marl Pit Road, Middletown, DE 19709, (302) 378-2102.

Crops:	Strawberries, tomatoes, turnips.
Season, Hours:	Mid-June through November. Call ahead for hours.
Directions:	From Route 896/301 turn east on Route 429. Lovett's is the second farm on the left.

☐ Perry Farms
P.O. Box 162, Odessa, DE 19330, (302) 378-0603.

Crops:	Asparagus.
Season, Hours:	Mid-April to mid-June. Call ahead for hours.
Directions:	Route 299, just 200 feet west of Route 13 in Odessa.

☐ Powell Farm
4525 South du Pont Highway, Townsend, DE 19934, (302) 378-7011.

Crops:	Strawberries, lima and string beans, tomatoes.
Season, Hours:	Year round, daily from 8 a.m. to 8 p.m.
Directions:	Route 13 in Blackbird, Delaware.

☐ Gerald Zeh Farm
R.D. 2, P.O. Box 731, Middletown, DE 19709, (302) 378-2840.

Crops:	Strawberries.
Season, Hours:	Late May to mid-June. Call ahead for hours.
Directions:	Route 301; 4 miles south of Middletown, turn east at the Texaco station. It's the third house on the right, 1 mile down the road.

Kent County

City of Dover

The Green
State Street and Bank Lane, Dover, DE

Laid out in 1722 in accordance with William Penn's orders, this square is the hub of state government now as it has been since the 18th century. In its early days, it served as a market for farmers and a place where hawkers sold their wares. Slaves were bought and sold here in spite of a growing abolitionist sentiment. Delaware's Continental regiment committed themselves to service in the Revolutionary War on the green in 1775. In July 1776, the Declaration of Independence was read to the public, sparking a celebration in which a portrait of George III, taken from a nearby tavern, was burned in a bonfire on the green by local militiamen. The buildings that surround the green encapsulate the history of Dover, the state capital and Kent County seat.

Delaware State Museum
316 Governor's Avenue, Dover, DE. (302) 736-3260. Tuesday through Saturday, 10 a.m. to 4:30 p.m.; Sunday, 1:30 to 4:30 p.m. Free.

A complex of three buildings, the State Museum is an entertaining and educational spot for a family visit. The first building, a former Presbyterian

An early sound equipment exhibit at
Johnson Memorial Building

church, now features changing exhibits on different periods of history and life in Delaware. Household furnishings and costumes from the Victorian era are currently on display. The 1880 Gallery, the second building, houses a series of shops and crafts exhibits that depict the occupations of Delawareans during the 1800s and 1900s. Domestic lifestyles and professions such as pharmacy, printing, blacksmithing, cordwaining, and weaving are highlighted. Live demonstrations on the printing press and loom will intrigue the little ones. Kids find the third building, the Johnson Memorial, fascinating. Designed as a 1920s Victrola dealer's store, it's a tribute to Eldridge Reeves Johnson, a Delaware native who was the inventor and founder of the Victor Talking Machine Company, the corporate predecessor of RCA. After learning about early recording artists and the Victor Company's famous trademark puppy Nipper, visitors hear original story, music, and physical exercise program recordings on the old-fashioned sound equipment. It's a real novelty to this generation's high-tech youngsters.

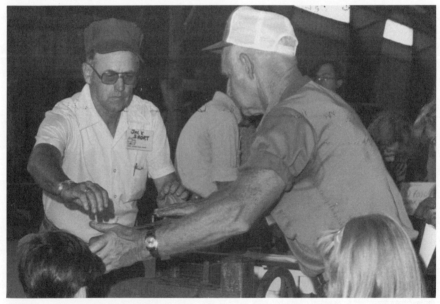

Cider-pressing demonstration at the Delaware Agricultural Museum

Dover Heritage Trail
P.O. Box 1628, Dover, DE. (302) 678-2040. May through October: Thursday, 10 a.m. Other times by reservation. Children 5 to 17, $1; children under 5, free; adults, $3.50.

The well-trained volunteer guides of Dover Heritage Trail, the official hostesses of Dover, provide an informative, entertaining walking tour of the Dover Historic District that makes for a very pleasant family outing. Experts at captivating young audiences, they tell stories of people, places, and events in Delaware history as they march the troops from the Margaret O'Neill Visitors Center where the tour originates, through the Hall of Records, Legislative Hall, Christ Church, and the Green. Youngsters learn about Delaware's curious boundaries: two straight lines, a curved line, and a wiggly line on the water. They sit in the seat of a state senator or representative while being introduced to the legislative process through the story of the ladybug, Delaware's state insect. They learn how Delaware patriot Caesar Rodney helped get the Declaration of Independence off the ground and why Delaware is known as the first state. The tour's grand finale is a visit to Delaware's replica of the Liberty Bell. Unlike the original in Philadelphia, this one can be rung. This is the way to get the most out of your Dover visit.

Hall of Records
Duke of York Street, Dover, DE. (302) 736-4266. Tuesday through Friday, 8:30 a.m. to 4:15 p.m.; Saturday, 8:30 a.m. to 3:45 p.m. Free.

The Hall of Records houses all the state's public archives, many of which focus on Delaware's ratification of the U.S. Constitution. One of the most interesting items on display is the Royal Charter granted by Charles II to James, Duke of York, for the territory that later became Delaware. While all this may be a little esoteric for the bambinos, older kids with some appreciation for history will find it appealing.

Legislative Hall
Legislative Avenue, Dover, DE. (302) 736-4101. Monday through Friday, 8:30 a.m. to 4:30 p.m.; weekends, by appointment. Free.

The perfect place for an up-close and personal civics lesson, Legislative Hall is where the state's General Assembly meets. The state senate and

Delaware's replica of the Liberty Bell

house of representative facilities are located on the first floor. The governor's working offices are located on the second. Canvases of former Delaware governors and World War II heroes are displayed throughout.

Margaret O'Neill Visitor Center
Court and Federal streets, Dover, DE. (302) 736-4266. Monday through Saturday, 8:30 a.m. to 4:30 p.m.; Sunday, 1:30 to 4:30 p.m. Free.

Make this your first stop in Dover. The friendly and helpful staff at the Visitor Center know their stuff and will gladly offer information on the places and events in city of Dover and Kent County. While you're there, check out the changing exhibits and view the slide show on the local historic sites. It's the best way to get your bearings on what's doing in and around Dover.

Old Christ Church
South State and Water streets, Dover, DE. (302) 734-5731. Weekdays, 10 a.m. to 4 p.m. Free.

Nestled in an ancient grove of trees, this quiet colonial church was built in 1734. Caesar Rodney, a Delaware patriot famous for his roles as founding father of state government, Revolutionary War leader, and signer of the Declaration of Independence, is buried in the adjacent graveyard.

Old State House
The Green, Dover, DE. (302) 736-4266 or 736-5316. Tuesday through Saturday, 10 a.m. to 4:40 p.m.; Sunday, 1:30 to 4:30 p.m. Free.

Said to be the second oldest state house in the country, the Old State House was built in 1792 on the site of a 1722 courthouse as the headquarters for state and county government. Although state government activities have, for the most part, been shifted to Legislative Hall, it remains the official capitol of Delaware. The building houses the governor's presentation and ceremonial office, and an 18th-century courtroom and legislative chambers. Guided tours of the Old State House begin at the Visitors Center. Special services for children include "Ghost Marks of the Past," an educational reserved program designed for elementary school students. Conducted by guides from the Delaware Bureau of Museums and Historic

Old State House

Sites, the tour includes a slide show, a building tour, and the reading of phrases from period manuscripts. After the formal presentation, the kids play detective, looking for hidden architectural and archeological "ghost marks" on the building and the grounds.

Woodburn

151 Kings Highway, Dover, DE. (302) 736-5656. September through June: Saturday, 2:30 to 4:30 p.m. Free.

Where does the state's chief executive hang his hat and in what style does he live? Your budding politicos can find the answers to these questions at Woodburn. Built in 1791, this handsome Georgian residence, once a station on the Underground Railroad, has been the official governor's mansion since 1966. Hours of operation can vary from what's listed above. To avoid disappointment, call ahead before your visit.

Suburban Dover

Delaware Agricultural Museum

866 North Du Pont Highway, Dover, DE. (302) 734-1618. April through December: Tuesday through Saturday, 10 a.m. to 4 p.m.; Sunday, 1 to 4 p.m. Children 10 to 16, $2; children under 10, free; adults, $3.

Old MacDonald had a farm and so does the Delaware Agricultural Museum. It's a place kids love to visit. In the main exhibit building they'll see a collection of tractors, horse-drawn equipment, and exhibits on poultry and dairy farming. A "please touch" room, filled with replicas of objects used on the farm and in the farmhouse, was specially created for children. Outside on the grounds visitors peruse a variety of structures that represent 200 years of agrarian life in the First State including a farmhouse, an outhouse, a granary, a wagon shed, a pig pen, a barn, a corn house, a meat house, a blacksmith and wheelwright shop, a schoolhouse, and a waterwheel-powered mill that performs grain-grinding and timber-sawing functions. The museum is a great destination any time during its operating season, but at planting and harvesting times live demonstrations illustrate in more detail the seasonal work and recreational activities of the farm community. Livestock raising, planting, food preserving, cooking, basket and broom making, weaving, quilting, blacksmithing, and cider-making activities are often part of the program in the spring or fall. Pack a picnic to enjoy on the tables the museum provides. Bring a stroller or backpack if you've got little ones. It's a bit of a hike from building to building.

Dover Air Force Base

Route 113, south of Dover, DE. (302) 678-6454. June through August: Third Saturday of the month, 10 a.m. to 2 p.m. Free.

A common sight in the skies over Dover is the C-5 Galaxy, the largest military cargo plane in the Western world. The C-5s and other military planes are flying to and from Dover Air Force Base. Most Americans know the base only through its saddest function—as a temporary repository for the remains of military and civilian men and women tragically killed in such places as Beruit or Jonestown, and on the doomed Challenger space shuttle. It also has an upbeat side. At the base's monthly summer open house, your would-be pilots can see the C-5 along with *Shoo Shoo, Baby,* a World War II B-17 under restoration at the Air Base Museum.

Kent County Beyond Dover

Bombay Hook National Wildlife Refuge and Allee House
Route 9, Smyrna, DE. (302) 653-9345. Driving Tour Route: Daily, sunrise to sunset; $3 per car. Refuge Visitor Center: Daily, 8 a.m. to 4 p.m., except summer weekends; free. Allee House: Weekends, 2 to 5 p.m.; free.

Bombay Hook, located right on the North Atlantic flyway, is definitely for the birds. It's the perfect place to meet migrating and resident feathered friends such as blue heron, Canada geese, snow geese, osprey, quail, and a wide variety of waterfowl. White-tailed deer and other four-footed critters native to this part of the state can also be observed. Begin your visit at the orientation center where you'll view exhibits on the local flora and fauna and learn about the refuge system at work in the park. For a reasonable fee, families may drive through the open fields and around the expansive pond and see the wildlife from the comfort of the car. For more adventure-some visitors, there are four different mile-long hiking trails. Whichever route you choose, bring the camera and binoculars. You and the kids won't want to miss the animal antics seen from the ground or one of the refuge's three observation towers.

Plan your visit for the fall, winter, or early spring. Summer is mosquito season. Picnic facilities are available. If you seek the refuge of the refuge on a weekend, stop by the Allee House. It's an early-18th-century country house owned, restored, and maintained by the state.

Island Field Museum and Research Center
Route 113, South Bowers Beach, DE. (302) 335-5395. April through November: Tuesday through Saturday, 10 a.m. to 4:30 p.m.; Sunday, 1:30 to 4:30 p.m. Free.

This unusual museum of anthropology and archeology houses and pre-serves an ancient Native American burial site. The archeological excavation is actually part of the self-guided tour. Some displays touch on the cultural

A costumed interpreter at the John Dickinson Plantation

history of the Indians in Delaware and the mid-Atlantic region. Others explain the principles and methods of anthropology and archeology used to explore the lives of ancient peoples and their cultures. Visitors are welcome to try their hand at an ancient grinding stone, used by Delaware's first citizens for pulverizing nuts and seeds. The regular self-guided tour is fascinating to older children. Specialized reserved tours for groups of children 10 years or older can be arranged.

John Dickinson Plantation
Kitts Hummock Road off Route 113, 8 miles south of Dover. (302) 736-4266. Tuesday through Saturday, 10 a.m. to 4:30 p.m.; Sunday, 1:30 to 4:30 p.m. Free.

John Dickinson, who served terms as governor of Delaware and Pennsylvania, is famous for his role in the American Revolution and for the part he played in Delaware's ratification of the U.S. Constitution. As a young boy he lived in this home, then known as Poplar Hall, a fashionable Georgian dwelling built by his father in 1740. Gutted by fire from a chimney spark in 1804, the house was quickly and lovingly rebuilt at Dickinson's direction. Furnished in period antiques, the house was opened as a museum by the state in the mid-1950s. Through a state grant, given in celebration of the 200th anniversary of Delaware's ratification of the U.S. Constitution, many of the plantation's outbuildings have been researched and are now being reconstructed based on archeological study. When the project is complete, the plantation tour will encompass the house along with a smokehouse, corn crib, stable, well, cider press, feed barn, granary, and a formal, Colonial Revival garden—all recreated to reflect the late-18th-century period.

The public is welcome to observe the project in progress. Seeing an ongoing restoration is a new and different learning experience for most children. The guides are happy to offer interesting tidbits on what the archeological studies turned up as well as information on each building's construction and function. "Plantation Life," a special reserved tour for children's groups, acquaints young visitors with John Dickinson as a historical figure, describes 18th-century domestic activities such as food preservation and cooking, and introduces kids to the farming practices of the period.

Kent County "Pick Your Own" Farms

□ American Beauty Produce
R.D. 2, P.O. Box 1498, Smyrna, DE 19977, (302) 653-6460.

Crops:	Strawberries.
Season, Hours:	Mid-May to the end of June. Call ahead for hours.
Directions:	Go west about 2 miles on County Road 90 (Sunnyside Road) off Route 13. It's the last farm on the right before you reach the railroad tracks.

□ Bobola Farms
R.D. 2, P.O. Box 326A, Dover, DE 19901, (302) 492-3367.

Crops:	Strawberries.
Season, Hours:	Mid-May to mid-June. Call ahead for hours.
Directions:	Route 8, 5 miles west of Dover.

☐ Eden Hill Farm
West North Street, Dover, DE 19901, (302) 734-0456.

Crops:	Pumpkins.
Season, Hours:	October, Monday through Saturday. Call ahead for hours.
Directions:	Between U.S. Cold Storage and General Foods.

☐ Antone Ficner Farm
R.D. 4, P.O. Box 271, Dover, DE 19901, (302) 674-4677.

Crops:	Strawberries.
Season, Hours:	Mid-May to mid-June. Call ahead for hours.
Directions:	From Route 13 turn east at the stoplight at Cheswold onto Route 42 and travel 2 miles.

☐ Hrupsa Farm
P.O. Box 192A, Harrington, DE, (302) 284-4804.

Crops:	Strawberries, sweet corn.
Season, Hours:	Mid-May through Labor Day, seven days a week from 8 a.m. to sunset.
Directions:	From Route 13 travel west on Route 12 to County Road 281. Take a left to Masten's Corner and a right on County Road 58 to County Road 271, where you turn left. Hrupsa's is the first farm on the left.

☐ Malenfant Farm
R.D. 1, P.O. Box 239, Marydel, DE 19964, (302) 492-8715.

Crops:	Strawberries, peas, lima beans.
Season, Hours:	Summer months. Call ahead for hours.
Directions:	Located at the intersection of County Roads 207 and 208.

☐ **Mason-Dixon Honey Farm**
R.D. 2, P.O. Box 306, Milford, DE 19963, (302) 422-4668.

Crops:	Peaches (Bell of Georgia, Elberta, Blake, Loring, Hail Haven, Golden Jubilee, and Red Haven).
Season, Hours:	July through September, daily, 8 a.m. to 7 p.m.
Directions:	Off Route 113 at Lynch Heights on Route 19 (Thompsonville Road) north of Milford.

☐ **Simpson Farm**
P.O. Box 79A, Houston, DE 19954, (302) 422-8807.

Crops:	Strawberries, lima beans, watermelons, cantaloupes, tomatoes, okra.
Season, Hours:	June through August, daily from 9 a.m. to sunset.
Directions:	County Road 384 between Houston and Williamsville.

☐ **T.A. Farms**
Rt. 1, P.O. Box 162A, Camden-Wyoming, DE 19934, (302) 493-3030.

Crops:	Strawberries, sweet corn, okra, tomatoes, pumpkins, sweet peppers.
Season, Hours:	Mid-May through October. Call ahead for hours.
Directions:	From Route 13 near Dover take Route 10 west to Petersburg. Take a right onto County Road 214 and a left onto County Road 207. It's the first farm on the left.

☐ **Warner Enterprises**
R.D. 2, P.O. Box 73A, Milford, DE 19963, (302) 422-9506.

Crops:	Strawberries, peas, potatoes, peppers, lima and green beans, beets, collards, turnips, kale, spinach, pumpkins, mums.
Season, Hours:	Daily, April through December, 9 a.m. to 5:30 p.m.
Directions:	County Road 406 near the intersection of Routes 113 and 1.

☐ **Warren Farm**
Loblolly Acres, P.O. Box 85, Woodside, DE 19980, (302) 284-9255.

Crops:	Chrysanthemums.
Season, Hours:	August 20 to October 31. Call ahead for hours.
Directions:	From Route 13 take County Road 30 to Woodside. Take a left on County Road 210 and look for the sign for Loblolly Acres.

☐ **William Wothers Farm**
R.D. 3, P.O. Box 324, Felton, DE 19943, (302) 284-9840.

Crops:	Strawberries.
Season, Hours:	Mid-May to mid-June, daily, 8 a.m. to 5 p.m.
Directions:	Route 13 at Canterbury, Delaware.

Pennsylvania

Pennsylvania's history is American history, particularly along the Delaware River Valley. In Philadelphia, home of Independence National Historic Park, families can relive together the important events of our past that have shaped our future at such places as Independence Hall, Franklin Court, and Liberty Bell Pavilion. The fifth largest city in the nation, Philadelphia also offers its residents and visitors a superb collection of art and science museums. The Philadelphia Zoological Gardens, commonly known in this region as "the Zoo," is the oldest in the nation.

In the counties that surround Philadelphia, agriculture is not only a mainstay of the regional economy but an aesthetic asset that contributes to the quality of life. The farms of the Delaware Valley provide a feast for the soul, eyes, ears, and stomach. In addition to its fieldstone and white-washed farmhouses and barns, its pastures and fields, the open country-side of the Delaware Valley is also dotted with parks, historic sites, and modern-day amusements and attractions that provide children and adults with unique opportunities for discovery, education, and just plain fun.

A fantasy fountain spurts water in mushroom shapes at Longwood's Children's Garden.

Bucks County

Southern Bucks County

Pennsbury Manor
400 Pennsbury Memorial Lane, Morrisville, PA. (215) 946-0400. Tuesday through Saturday, 9 a.m. to 5 p.m.; Sunday, noon to 5 p.m. Children 6 to 18, $1; children under 6, free; adults, $2.50.

These are the digs of Pennsylvania's namesake and numero uno of colonial history, William Penn. While a lot of 18th-century history and life is interpreted in and around this part of the state, little remains of the 17th. Pennsbury Manor is a re-creation of the original estate of William Penn built in 1683. The manor house, authentically constructed and furnished in every detail, stands on the original's foundations. The 17th-century life and times of William Penn, who was America's foremost Quaker, a diplomat, statesman, and founder of the state of Pennsylvania, are discovered in the residence, outbuildings, and gardens that make up this gracious but elegantly simple English estate. A 20-minute slide presentation begins the tour and informs visitors about Penn and his contributions to colonial history. It also covers the 1938 reconstruction of this riverside plantation.

In addition to the main house, visitors tour the bake and brew house, smokehouse, icehouse, plantation manager's office, and stable. Domestic animal breeds typical of the era graze in the farmyard. In the classic flower

High-tech kids love the Computer Gallery at Sesame Place.

garden, orchard, and medicinal herb and vegetable garden, plant species common in 17th-century England are cultivated. The guides are astute about including children in their repartee as they move tourists through the various exhibits.

Picnic facilities are available, and strollers or backpacks are recommended for little ones touring with adults. A reserved group program for children includes a specially scripted plantation tour along with 17th-century activities such as quill pen writing, games, and wool carding and spinning.

Sesame Place

New Oxford Valley Road off U.S. Route 1, Langhorne, PA. (215) 752-7070. Mid-May to early September: Daily, 10 a.m. to 5 p.m. Call ahead for extended summer hours and fall weekend schedules. Children over 2, $13.95; children under 2, free; adults, $11.95.

From toddlers to grade schoolers, kids go gaga at this indoor-outdoor amusement and educational attraction. The Sesame Street Neighborhood allows children to step into a re-creation of the famous TV studio set with Oscar's Garage, the Fix-it Shop, Mr. MacIntosh's Fruit Stand, and the Fire Station. They also meet many of their favorite Muppets. At the Rainbow Pyramid and Shadow Room they discover the wonders of science—a ball balanced on an invisible stream of air and shadows that stay put even when the objects casting them are removed. Big Bird's Court is a must for little ones. Here they can jump, spin, slide, and whirl in safety. The Computer Gallery beckons kids to participate in over 50 different computer games and activities.

Be sure to bring bathing suits. Water rides and slides are a Sesame Place mainstay. There are changing rooms for kids and adults. Plan to spend a good three hours. Bring a picnic or eat at the park's Food Factory or Sandwich Shop. Pack a stroller for the small fry and you'll save time moving from one activity to the next.

Washington Crossing Historic Park

Routes 32 and 532, Washington Crossing, PA. (215) 493-4076. Monday through Saturday, 9 a.m. to 5 p.m.; Sunday, noon to 5 p.m. Park: Children 6 to 17, 50¢; children under 6, free; adults, $1.50. Bowman Hill Tower: Children 3 to 12, 50¢; children under 3, free; adults, $2.

Cookie Monster greets two small visitors at Sesame Place.

For children studying American history, this 500-acre state park is a "must visit" destination. It was from this site that George Washington and company crossed the icy Delaware River on Christmas night, 1776, to launch their attack on Hessian-occupied Trenton and changed the course of the Revolutionary War.

Begin your tour at the Memorial Building where you see a half-hour orientation film and view a replica of Emanual Leutze's famous painting, *Washington Crossing the Delaware*. After orientation, take the guided tour. It includes historic buildings in two sections of the park. The Thompson's

Mill section features the Thompson-Neely House, the riverside residence where General Washington and his senior men outlined the attack; the Thompson Mill Barn; and the Thompson Grist Mill, an operating water-powered grain mill restored to reflect operations in the mid-19th century. In the McConkey's Ferry Section see the McConkey Ferry Inn, where Washington and his staff held the final strategy meeting prior to making the crossing; Durham Boat House, where reproductions of the vessels used in the crossing are displayed; and Homewood, the house of Mahlon K. Taylor, founder of Taylorsville, which was later renamed Washington's Crossing.

Explore the park's Bowman Hill section on your own. It includes a 100-acre wildflower preserve, miles of hiking trails, and a 110-foot lookout tower. The view from the top is a 14-mile expanse of the Delaware Valley. Pack a lunch. Picnic tables are available at scenic locations throughout the park.

Village of New Hope

The little village of New Hope is worth a mention in and of itself. It stands on a tract of land originally granted to an English settler by William Penn in 1681. Famous for its ferry in the 18th century, the settlement took the name Coryell's Ferry, after the enterprising gentleman who ran the boats back and forth to New Jersey during the time of the American Revolution. Industry grew in the community with the establishment of two flourishing mills. When the mills were destroyed by fire in 1790, the local economy was devastated. After they were rebuilt, the proprietor dubbed them the New Hope Mills.

The name stuck and still has relevance today, particularly for the aspiring performing and visual artists, craft artisans, and imaginative restaurateurs who now ply their skills in this energetic and creative community. Synonymous with New Hope is the Bucks County Playhouse, training ground and refuge for many of the country's finest actors. From April through December, the Playhouse Company presents a series of hit Broadway plays and musicals, some appropriate for young audiences. Painting, sculpture, and craft galleries abound as do quaint inns and notable eateries. Many are "kid-friendly." The New Hope Mule Barge and local steam railway are custom-made family attractions. A full family day or weekend could happily be spent in this appealing river town.

Bucks County Playhouse

70 South Main Street, New Hope, PA. (215) 862-2041. April through December. (Call to see who and what is playing.) Matinee: $18 to $22.50 per seat; evening performances: $20 to $25 per seat.

Dubbed by a critic "the unofficial state theater of Pennsylvania," the Bucks County Playhouse consistently brings to its audiences an exciting blend of nationally recognized talent in its annual season of plays and musicals. Less expensive and stuffy than Broadway, its matinees give kids exposure to professional theater in a comfortable atmosphere.

New Hope Barge Company

South Main Street, New Hope, PA. (215) 862-2842. April: Wednesday, Saturday, and Sunday, 1, 2, 3, and 4:30 p.m. May 1 through October 15: Daily, 11:30 a.m., 1, 2, 3, 4:30, and 6 p.m. October 16 through November 15: Wednesday, Saturday, Sunday, 11:30 a.m., 1, 2, 3, and 4:30 p.m. Children 12 and under, $3.75; adults, $6.50.

Want to see Bucks County from a different vantage point? This mule-drawn barge is just the ticket and something children simply love. On a one-hour ride down the Delaware Canal, one of the few preserved canals in the United States, passengers pass colonial cottages, artists' workshops, romantic gardens, and a restored steam railroad. During the summer season, a musician and historian entertain barge riders with songs and tales of life and history along this manmade waterway, begun in 1827 and completed in 1832.

New Hope Steam Railway and Museum

32 West Bridge Street, New Hope, PA. (215) 862-2707. May through October: Saturdays and holidays, 1:30, 3:30 p.m.; Sundays, 11:30 a.m., 1:30, 3:30 p.m. Children, $3; adults, $5.

Hop aboard for a nine-mile, 1½ hour round trip back to the glory days of steam railroading. The trip begins at the New Hope Station, a newly restored Victorian structure with a distinctive witch's hat turret. As the train steams by on the leisurely nine-mile trip from New Hope to Lahaska, passengers will cross the curved trestle bridge featured in the vintage movie serials, *Perils of Pauline,* and feel the power of the locomotive as it pulls them up the 2 percent grade of Solebury Mountain. Woodlands, rock cuts,

New Hope Mule Barge

and the open countryside are also part of the view along the railway's trackage, once owned by the North East Pennsylvania Railroad. Arrive before boarding time for a look at the railroad's rolling stock exhibits, which include three steam locomotives, a Baldwin diesel, a railway post office car, a parlor-club car, two trolley cars, and a caboose. Railroading memorabilia exhibits, a souvenir shop, and the ticket counter are housed in a wooden baggage car built in 1906. Kids of all ages will love the trip as will the adults who accompany them.

Old Franklin Print Shop
Main and Ferry streets, New Hope, PA. (215) 862-2956. Monday through Saturday: 10 a.m. to 5 p.m.; Sunday, 1 to 5 p.m. Free.

If your kids want to see their names in print, the Old Franklin Print Shop offers the opportunity. With his 1860 Washington Hand Press, the master printer will personalize any number of humorous, old-fashioned pre-printed posters, newspaper headlines, awards, citations, licenses, or book covers with the name of your choice as he demonstrates word processing as it once was.

Central Bucks County

Moravian Pottery and Tile Works
Swamp Road (Route 313), Doylestown, PA. (215) 345-6722. Monday through Sunday, 10 a.m. to 5 p.m. Children 7 to 17, $1; children under 7, free; adults, $2.

This living-history museum is in the business of producing ceramic tiles in much the same way as was done nearly 100 years ago under the direction of Henry Chapman Mercer, the Victorian gentleman who founded and built the enterprise. Kids enjoy following the self-guided tour, observing the various steps in this creative manufacturing process. The Tile Works is part of the Mercer Mile, which includes Fonthill, Mr. Mercer's estate, and the Mercer Museum, featuring exhibits of his vast collection of early American tools. Mercer's house and museum are better saved for an all-adult visit.

Quarry Valley Farm
Street Road, Lahaska, PA. (215) 794-5882. April through December: Daily, 10 a.m. to 5 p.m. Children under 12, $3; adults, $3.50.

A wonderful, low-key destination, Quarry Valley Farm is centered around the remains of an old quarry that supplied colonial farmers with the lime they used to fertilize their fields. In the late 18th century, a farmhouse and blacksmith shop were added when the quarry became a working farm.

Now opened for visitors, the farm is a great spot for a few hours of wholesome fun and a history lesson that is enthusiastically given and well received. Housed in the barn is a collection of "please touch" tools and implements—wheelbarrows, rakes, and plows—that kept an 18th-century farm running smoothly. In the hayloft, a little unbridled shouting and jumping is not only permitted but encouraged. Kids can saddle up and ride a Shetland pony, see how a cow is milked, pet Miss Piggy (a 500-pound porker), and feed the farm's sheep, goats, chickens, and ducks. The helpful, friendly farm tour guides add to the ambiance of this pleasant and interesting setting.

Bucks County "Pick Your Own" Farms

☐ **Fairview Farm**

P.O. Box 133, Pineville, PA, (215) 598-3257.

Crops:	Peas, strawberries, lima beans.
Season, Hours:	Call ahead for crop reports and hours.
Directions:	Located just off Route 413 on Pineville Road, midway between Newtown and Doylestown.

☐ **None Such Farms**

P.O. Box 177, Buckingham, PA, (215) 794-7742.

Crops:	Green beans, strawberries, pumpkins.
Season, Hours:	Call ahead for crop reports and hours.
Directions:	One-half mile south of Buckingham on Route 263.

☐ **Shelly and Hellerick Farm**

R.D. 5, Doylestown, PA, (215) 766-8388.

Crops:	Strawberries, pumpkins.
Season, Hours:	Late May through October. Call ahead for hours.
Directions:	Route 611, 6 miles north of Doylestown.

☐ **Paul C. Shelmire Farm**

510 Mill Road, Quakertown, PA, (215) 536-5182.

Crops:	Strawberries, string and lima beans.
Season, Hours:	May through September. Call ahead for hours.
Directions:	Take Route 309 to Route 663 to Milford Square Pike. Follow Hillcrest Road to Mill Road.

☐ **Solly Brothers Farm**

707 Almshouse Road, Ivyland, PA, (215) 357-2850.

Crops:	Strawberries, string beans, pumpkins.
Season, Hours:	June through October. Call ahead for hours.
Directions:	Route 332, 1.5 miles west of Richboro.

☐ Styer Orchards
R.D. 1, P.O. Box 250, Woodbourne Road, Langhorne, PA, (215) 757-7646.

Crops:	Strawberries.
Season, Hours:	Mid-May to mid-June.
Directions:	1.5 miles west of Oxford Valley Mall on Woodbourne Road.

☐ Wadin Tree Farm
Smithtown Road, Pipersville, PA, (215) 766-8123.

Crops:	Christmas trees.
Season, Hours:	Late November through December 23. Call ahead for hours.
Directions:	4.5 miles east of Pipersville off Dark Hollow Road.

☐ Tuckamony Farm
R.D. 1, P.O. Box 263, New Hope, PA, (215) 297-5054.

Crops:	Christmas trees.
Season, Hours:	Call ahead for dates and hours.
Directions:	Route 263, 2 miles north of Peddler's Village.

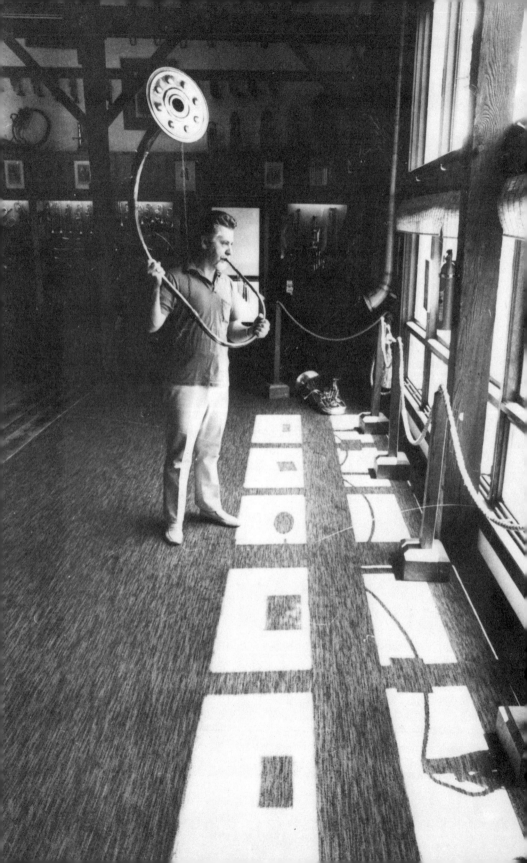

Chester County

Brandywine Valley

Barnes Brinton House
Route 1, Chadds Ford, PA. (215) 388-7376. June through August: Saturday and Sunday, 10 a.m. to 5 p.m. Children, 50¢; adults, $1.

Costumed guides explain the furnishings and functions of this 1714 brick tavern building. Live demonstrations of early 18th-century home arts and crafts such as candle-making, spinning, weaving, and sewing, and open-hearth cooking and baking are part of the presentation.

Hibernia Park and Mansion
Off Route 340, Wagontown, PA. (215) 384-0290. **Park:** *Year round, daily, 9 a.m. to 5 p.m.; free.* **Mansion:** *June through August, Sunday, 1 to 4 p.m.; $1 per person.*

Located on the west branch of the Brandywine, Hibernia was once the center of a prosperous ironworks. Guarding the gate to the ironmaster's home are two handsome lion heads. Inside, hostesses describe the the life and work of the company owner and his workers as they guide visitors through rooms of Victorian furnishings and decorative arts. House tours are offered

A guide demonstrates how a rare antique horn is played at the Streitwieser Trumpet Museum

only at the times specified above, but other remnants of the old industrial community are visible year round. They include Hibernia Church and five original worker's cottages. This old community is set amidst 800 acres of meadows and wooded glens. A stocked creek and pond provide challenging fishing to young anglers. Numerous trails will please the hikers in your group. Picnic and play equipment is also available, and tent and trailer camping hook-up sites may be reserved.

Longwood Gardens

Route 1, Kennett Square, PA. (215) 388-6741. Daily, 9 a.m. to 6 p.m. Call for schedule of extended evening hours during the summer and at Christmastime. Children 6 to 14, $1.50; children under 6, free; adults, $6.

Everybody doesn't like something, but nobody doesn't like Longwood Gardens, the estate of the late industrialist P.S. du Pont. Anyone from babbling babies to professional horticulturists can find a lot to love about this 350-acre paradise of indoor and outdoor gardens. Outside visitors will find carefully clipped hedges, flowering shrubs, towering trees, water gardens, a

**Young visitors enjoy Longwood Gardens'
indoor and outside flowering bulb
displays in the spring.**

lily pond, and artfully arranged plantings of annual and perennial flowers. During the summer, a five-acre fountain garden shimmers with color during evening fountain displays. When visitors attend one of Longwood's many performing arts productions in the 2,100-seat outdoor theatre, a curtain of illuminated water spurting from fountain jets separates the stage from the audience.

Inside the heated glass conservatory with its adjacent greenhouses, visitors can enjoy four acres of blooming flora at any time of the year. During the dreary days of late January and February, narcissus and tulips displayed in the glass house give visitors hope that spring will come. When fall arrives, mum's the word inside the conservatory. During the autumn months through Thanksgiving, 15,000 brilliantly hued chrysanthemum plants fill every nook and cranny. Christmastime is also special. The conservatory is resplendent with red, pink, and white poinsettias, various hollies, and evergreen wreaths and trees. Outdoors, 30,000 decorative lights sparkle in yuletide displays throughout the property.

Tailor-made for the bambinos, Longwood's Children's Garden is another indoor exhibit. Filled with opportunities to smell, touch, discover, climb, and view nature's marvels, the Children's Garden is a spot packed with

Kids love the sights, sounds and smells of Longwood's new Children's Garden.

plenty of do's and very few don'ts. It is home to a family of topiary bears and two reclining giraffes. Also featured are a tree house, a maze, a tea garden, and mushroom-shaped fountains.

If seeing all this greenery makes you hungry, visit Longwood's Terrace Restaurant, where both table service and cafeteria-style dining are available at lunchtime. If you are feeling ambitious, brown bag it. Picnics are permitted in certain outside areas. Be sure to remember a stroller or backpack if you're bringing babies or toddlers. You'll want to cover a lot of ground.

Newcomen Museum
412 Newcomen Road, Exton, PA. (215) 363-6600. Monday through Friday, 9 a.m. to 5 p.m. Free.

If cabin fever is getting the better of you and the kids, try blowing off a little steam at the Newcomen Museum. This nifty little spot houses quite an impressive collection of working steam engines and their electrically powered scale-model equivalents. Named for Thomas Newcomen, an Cornish inventor who designed the first fire engine in 1712, the museum features examples of his work along with stationary, marine, locomotive, and automotive steam engines that trace the evolution of steam power from the 18th to the 20th century.

Northbrook Canoe Company
Brandywine River at Northbrook, PA. (215) 793-2279 or 793-1553. April through October: Daily by reservation. Fees vary based on trip length and number of passengers.

This small and friendly enterprise wants to rent you a canoe, inner tube, or splash boat for a trip on the Brandywine River through the woodlands and open countryside of Chester County and northernmost New Castle County, Delaware. These reserved trips vary in length from an hour to all day. On the shorter runs, Northbrook employees will transport you and your canoe, tubes, or splash boat up-river to a put-in point, from whence you drift lazily downstream to their headquarters. The longer trips start at Northbrook and run down-river, where a Northbrook driver will meet you and your conveyance at a predetermined pick-up point for transport back to their docks. Their staff is happy to offer advice on trip lengths, based on the age and skill level of the kids you plan to bring along. Everyone in a Northbrook party must wear the life jackets provided.

Phillips Mushroom Place
Route 1, Kennett Square, PA. (215) 388-6082. Daily, 10 a.m. to 6 p.m. Children 7 to 12, 50¢; children under 7, free; adults, $1.25.

Kennett Square prides itself on being the mushroom capital of the world. You and the kids can follow the fable of this fungus at Phillips where you'll learn as much as you'll ever need to know about the mushroom. Video dioramas, slide shows, and still exhibits including a scale-model mushroom farm explain mushroom history, mystery, and lore. When the tour is over be sure to purchase a basket of captivating cap or beguiling button mushrooms. As with any fresh food, knowing the origin makes it all the tastier.

Northern Chester County

Hopewell Furnace
Route 345, 5 miles south of Birdsboro, PA. (215) 582-8773. Daily, 9 a.m. to 5 p.m. Children, free; adults, $1.

Technically Hopewell Furnace is located in Berks County, but it is part of French Creek State Park, which meanders over the line into Chester County. Regardless of location, it is a site worth a family stop. Begin at the Visitors Center with the 10-minute slide show, which serves as an orientation to this early-American industrial village. On the self-guided tour laid out clearly in brochure form, you'll visit the furnace complex which includes the cast house, the blacksmith shop, and the furnace itself. Here the iron-making process is demonstrated during the summer months. The life and work of the furnace owner and his employees are interpreted in the ironmaster's mansion and the workers' cottages. If you've completed the walking tour and have a question on any aspect of iron making, return to the visitors' center. Your answer will no doubt be found in one of the four short video presentations on blacksmithing, casting, molding, and charcoal making.

After visiting the furnace, enjoy the rest of this 6,000-acre state park. You can ride on its 57-acre lake in a rented canoe, paddleboat, or rowboat. Fishing is also allowed, so bring your young angler's rod. If you're planning a summer visit, pack swimming suits and a lunch. There's a pool and plenty of picnic facilities.

Streitwieser Trumpet Museum
Vaughan Road, Pottstown, PA. (215) 327-1351. By appointment; call ahead. Suggested donation for adults: $2.50.

Professor Harold Hill of *Music Man* fame would have had a field day here as would his young pupils. Over 600 instruments lead the big parade of exhibits, most of them trumpets of one kind or another. From primitive shell and animal-horn tooters to modern-day brass instruments, the museum's collection traces man's ever-present need for the sound of music. Demonstrations on museum horns are part of the presentation. It's worth the call.

Southern Chester County

Colonial Flying Corps Museum
New Garden Airport, Newark Road, Toughkenamon, PA. (215) 268-2048. Weekends, noon to 4 p.m. Unheated facility; closed in very cold weather. Children, $1; adults, $2.

A guide blows one of the 600 instruments at the Streitwieser Trumpet Museum.

If flight is your kid's fancy or fantasy, a visit to this little country museum located near a rural airstrip is worthwhile. Along with a beautifully maintained collection of small World War II–era aircraft, the museum features an antique car exhibit. The classic autos range from 80 to 30 years of age. Collector-quality bikes, motor- and pedal-powered, are also on view.

Herr's Snack Factory
Routes 131 and 272, Nottingham, PA. (800) 344-3777 and (215) 932-9330. Monday through Thursday: Tours at 9, 10, and 11 a.m. and 1 and 2 p.m. Call ahead; schedules change frequently. Free.

Are your kids big-time munchaholics? Take them on this factory tour and they'll think they've gone to heaven. There before their very eyes potatoes are sliced, cooked, and converted to chips. Pretzels are twisted and baked to a golden brown. Cheese curls and popcorn are puffed to perfection in a nifty hot-air machine. Corn and tortilla chips are shaken with Mexican seasoning and emerge ready for packing. They'll be ready and waiting to munch a bunch of the free samples distributed at the end of the tour.

Chester County "Pick Your Own" Farms

☐ Barnard's Orchards and Greenhouses
1079 Wawaset Road, Kennett Square, PA, (215) 347-2151.

Crops:	Apples, peaches.
Season, Hours:	June through October. Call ahead for hours.
Directions:	Route 842, 2 miles east of Unionville.

☐ Duncan's Farm Market
966 Valley Forge Road, Devon, PA, (215) 688-2786.

Crops:	Strawberries.
Season, Hours:	Mid-May to mid-June. Call ahead for hours.
Directions:	Take Route 202 to the Devon exit. Market is in first block off exit.

☐ Highland Orchards
1000 Thorndale Road, West Chester, PA, (215) 269-3494.

Crops:	Strawberries, raspberries, blueberries.
Season, Hours:	Call ahead for crop reports and hours.
Directions:	Just off Route 322.

☐ Northbrook Orchards
6 Northbrook Road, West Chester, PA, (215) 793-1210.

Crops:	Strawberries, peaches, apples.
Season, Hours:	Call ahead for crop reports and hours.
Directions:	Intersection of Route 842 and Northbrook Road, 5 miles west of West Chester.

☐ Nussex Farms
880 South Five Points Road, West Chester, PA, (215) 696-1133.

Crops:	Apples, sour cherries.
Season, Hours:	Call ahead for crop reports and hours.
Directions:	Routes 202 and 3 at Five Point Road.

☐ Wetherill Tree Farm
Beaver Hill Road, Chester Springs, PA, (215) 827-7227.

Crops:	Christmas trees.
Season, Hours:	November to December. Call ahead for hours.
Directions:	Ludwigs Corner, 1 mile northeast of the intersection of Routes 401 and 100.

☐ Woodward Farms
Route 52, Mendenhall, PA, (215) 388-6900.

Crops:	Apples, blueberries, peaches, pumpkins.
Season, Hours:	Call ahead for crop reports and hours.
Directions:	Just north of the Mendenhall railroad tracks off the southbound lane of Route 52.

Delaware County

Brandywine Valley

Brandywine Battlefield State Park
Route 1, Chadds Ford, PA. (215) 459-3342. Tuesday through Saturday, 9 a.m. to 5 p.m.; Sunday, noon to 5 p.m. Grounds: Free. Buildings and exhibits: Children 6 to 18, 50¢; children under 6, free; adults, $1.

This park is the site of one of the Revolutionary War's largest encampments, and commemorates the Battle of the Brandywine, fought just a mile away. Although the battle was lost by the colonials, their courageous stand attracted French support for the cause of independence. A tour of the park begins at the visitors' center, where a short slide presentation covers the battle and orients visitors. A small exhibit of Revolutionary War memorabilia is also on view. Then it's on to Washington's Headquarters and Lafayette's Quarters, two historic buildings that are interpreted by guides and used as vehicles to further describe the battle, how it was planned, and the lives and histories of the officers and soldiers who fought.

Pack a picnic. There are outdoor tables and benches. During the week in summer visitors can stay on the grounds until 8 p.m., but the buildings close at 5 p.m. The one-hour tour is perfect for pint-sized historians.

N. C. Wyeth's In the Crystal Depths *is one of the many paintings on view at the Brandywine River Museum.*

Brandywine River Museum

Route 1, Chadds Ford, PA. (215) 459-1900. Daily, 9:30 a.m. to 4:30 p.m. Children 6 to 18, $1.50; children under 6, free; adults, $3.

Located in a restored gristmill along the Brandywine, this museum presents the works of three generations of famous Wyeth family painters and others whose style is broadly linked to the Brandywine School, developed by artist and illustrator Howard Pyle nearly a century ago. Kids will find N.C. Wyeth's illustrations of cowboys, Indians, and *Treasure Island* pirates as fascinating as his grandson Jamie's out-sized and artful impression of a momma pig. Lunch and afternoon snacks are available in the museum's self-serve restaurant, which boasts a breathtaking view of the Brandywine. After your museum visit, take the mile-long nature walk through the museum's surrounding grounds. You'll understand why the regional landscape continues to spark the imaginations of visual artists.

Special children's programs and services include exceptional model train and doll displays at Christmastime and a reserved group program, "Art and the Environment," offered in the spring and fall. Geared to fourth, fifth, and sixth graders, the presentation illustrates the relationship of art

Kids are mesmerized by the Christmas model train exhibit at the Brandywine River Museum

to the landscape through its slide show, gallery tour, and river-trail hiking activities.

John Chad House

Route 100, Chadds Ford, PA. (215) 388-7376. June through August; Saturday and Sunday, 10 a.m. to 5 p.m. Children, 50¢; adults, $1.

Follow the trail from the Brandywine River Museum or drive up Route 100 to reach this quaint colonial cottage. Built in 1725 by the man who ran a small ferry along the Brandywine, the house features an open hearth and beehive oven where bread is baked and colonial home life is explained by a costumed interpreter.

Franklin Mint Museum

Route 1, Wawa, PA. (215) 459-6168. Tuesday through Saturday, 9:30 a.m. to 4:30 p.m.; Sunday, 1 to 4:30 p.m. Free.

Over 3,500 people, places, and historical events have been commemorated on coins, medals, and ingots and in the pewter, bronze, clay, and glass objects crafted at the Franklin Mint, the world's largest private minting operation. The mint's coin-shaped museum houses original works by American

The coin-shaped Franklin Mint Museum

artists such as Norman Rockwell and Andrew Wyeth. More important, it showcases examples of work created for limited-edition release to the public by the Franklin Mint's artists in a variety of art media. Little girls will find the heirloom doll display irresistible.

Newlin Mill Park

Route 1 and South Cheyney Road, Glen Mills, PA. (215) 459-2359. Grounds: Daily, 8 a.m. to dusk; free. Buildings, activities: Weekdays, 9 a.m. to 4 p.m.; weekends, 9 a.m. to 5 p.m.; children, 75¢; adults, $1.50.

This quaint little park is operated by a family foundation created by a ninth-generation descendant of Nicholas Newlin, an English emigré who received a patent for the land from William Penn in 1685. In the early 18th century, Nicholas's son Nathaniel built a stone gristmill and dam by the creek on the property and a home for the miller next door. When an interested ancestor purchased the property in 1957, he had the mill's great wooden cogs, gears, and pinions authentically restored to working order and grain was again ground. Shortly after that the house was restored to its 1739 appearance and a replica blacksmith shop was added. An ancient springhouse was relocated stone by stone over a fresh flowing spring on the property. A period log house with a large open hearth was then constructed.

For a fee, visitors to the park can tour the buildings, play tennis, or fish in the stocked millrace or ponds. Family picnicking and nature trail walks through the park's 140 acres of woodlands and fields are free.

1704 House

Oakland Road off Route 202, Dilworthtown, PA. (215) 692-4800. May through October: Tuesday, Thursday, and Saturday, 1 to 4 p.m. Children, 50¢; adults, $1.

The open grounds around this reconstructed Quaker home of medieval English design easily absorb the antics and energy of children. Inside, early furnishings and decorative arts are used as vehicles to describe the history and lives of the Brinton family, the home's early-18th-century occupants.

Central Delaware County

Colonial Pennsylvania Plantation

Ridley Creek State Park, Sycamore Mills Road, Media, PA. (215) 566-1725. April through November: Saturday and Sunday, 10 a.m. to 4 p.m. Children $1; adults, $2.

This working farm accurately depicts rural agrarian life as it really was in the 18th century, not a romanticized view backward through 20th-century eyes. It is unique in that its fields, farmhouse, barn, and springhouse have been left virtually unaltered by time. The museum staff is committed to authenticity. The period clothing they wear, the tools and implements they use, and the activities they demonstrate as they interpret the site for visitors are steeped in 18th-century reality. Even the barnyard animals—horses, cattle, sheep, and pigs—are now-rare breeds that were common to pre-Revolutionary Southeastern Pennsylvania.

The farm follows the philosophy of self-reliance. Flax, grown in the kitchen garden, is converted to linen on an early loom. The cloth is used for the hand-stitched period clothing worn by the interpreters. Some farm chores and tasks are demonstrated continuously, such as butter and cheese making, baking, cooking, and drawing well water. Others occur on a seasonal basis as they would have over two centuries ago. Wheat, barley, and rye fields are cultivated with a horse-drawn plow and planted by hand in the spring. The kitchen garden is planted with vegetable seed varieties common to the era, and herbs, which were used at the time more for medicinal purposes than for food seasoning. Sheep shearing is also part of the spring farming ritual. When the harvest is complete, interpreters prepare for the coming winter. Fall demonstrations include food preservation, candle and soap making, coloring wool with vegetable dyes, and spinning and weaving cloth. Visitors are welcome to pack a picnic and spend time at the plantation before or after the 1½ hour tour.

If you and the kiddos want the real scoop on how life in the country once was, this is the place to get it. Special services for children include one-, two-, and four-hour reserved group tours and workshops, each planned with the age and interest level of the children in mind.

*Children dressed in period clothing at the
Colonial Pennsylvania Plantation*

Delaware County Institute of Science

11 Veterans Square, Media, PA. (215) 566-3491. Monday, 9 a.m. to 1 p.m.; other times by appointment. Free.

This small institute is run by a group of dedicated and professional volunteers who are happy to share what they know with visitors of any age. Its collections of minerals, shells, Indian artifacts, and Delaware County birds and plants are explained with accuracy, folksy charm, and sensitivity to youthful audiences.

Linvilla Orchards

137 West Knowlton Road, Media, PA. (215) 876-7116. Daily, 10 a.m. to 6 p.m. Free.

Although Linvilla is mentioned as a "pick-your-own" farm, it deserves additional attention for its other events and activities. This 300-acre fruit and vegetable farm has as its focal point a Victorian octagonal barn. Originally used for dairy operations, it is now the farm's retail outlet for fresh produce, homemade baked goods, candy, cider, honey, and dairy products. The farm uses imagination in the way it blends commercial and educational interests. Visitors can pet pigs, puppies, horses, hens, geese, goats, rabbits, and turkeys, which are raised on the property along with tame white-tail deer. Kids can climb on old tractors or munch a sandwich in an area designated for play and picnicking.

Choosing a Linvilla pumpkin for Halloween has become a late fall tradition. In addition to selecting their own would-be jack-o-lantern, kids tour the orchard's Pumpkinland exhibits, a series of vignettes taken from local history, fairy tales, and television. The sight of a pumpkin-headed George Washington crossing the Delaware in a boat constructed of squashes is truly something to behold. Weekend hayrides are also available during September and October. Admission is charged for the 15-minute farm cart trip. In late November, an annual Thanksgiving display marks the end of another harvest season. Wreaths of every shape and description, a 12-foot nutcracker, and nativity sets from around the world are part of the orchard's Christmas presentation.

While Linvilla's approach is any- and everything but slick, it's a fun place for kids to visit. Bring some extra cash, and you'll be able to knock out some of the weekly grocery shopping while you're there.

Southern Delaware County

Family Fun Spot
Route 322, Aston, PA. (215) 485-1024. Memorial Day through Labor Day: daily, noon to 8:00 p.m. Water slide, ten rides, $4; Go-carts, three rides, $6; Miniature golf, $2.50 per person.

This probably won't ring an adult's chimes. It has no redeeming educational, historic, or general social value, but kids will love this water-slide recreation park. In addition to riding the slippery slopes of the slides, kids can drive go-carts and test the links on an 18-hole miniature golf course.

Thomas Leiper House
52 Avondale Road, Wallingford, PA. (215) 566-6365. April through December: Saturday and Sunday, 1 to 4 p.m. Children, 50¢; adults, $1.

This is the summer home of one of Philadelphia's first famous industrialists, Thomas Leiper. This colonial CEO came from Scotland to Virginia in the mid-1700s and observed the plantation operation of the tobacco industry. He left for Pennsylvania, where he founded a snuff mill, built a successful quarry business, and developed the state's first railroad, a series of horse-drawn cars used to transport his snuff and stone to the Delaware River for sale upstream in Philadelphia. Inside, visitors view the period furnishings of the anteroom, music room, dining room, and butler's pantry. Outside, they see the Security, or private bank, and the Necessary, or pre-Revolutionary powder room. Most important, they get a handle on the home and business life of an aspiring citizen of the 18th century.

Morton Mortenson Homestead
Route 420 and Darby Creek, Prospect Park, PA. (215) 583-7221. March through December: Wednesday to Saturday, 10 a.m. to 4 p.m.; Sunday, noon to 4 p.m. Children, 50¢; adults, $1.

The contributions of early Swedish settlers to colonial America are discovered at this log house, built in the late 17th century by Morton Mortenson. Reproduction Swedish peasant furniture is showcased in the three-room structure. Guides escort visitors through the parlor, used by the original occupants only on state occasions; the workroom; and the living room, where the family cooked, ate, and slept. The house is located on 2½ acres along the Darby Creek. Visitors are welcome to fish or picnic along the stream. The children's reserved group program includes a tour and hands-on activities such as butter churning, wool carding, and fire tending.

Caleb Pusey House
15 Race Street, Upland, PA. (215) 874-5665. July and August: Weekdays, 10 a.m. to 4 p.m. May through October: Weekends, 1 to 4 p.m. Children, 50¢; adults, $1.

One of Pennsylvania's oldest homes, Caleb Pusey House was built in 1683. Originally occupied by William Penn's mill manager, Caleb Pusey, the two-room structure houses a number of artifacts used in the 17th-century home and farm. One room features spinning wheels, an inside well, a set kettle used for brewing beer, and period lighting implements such as betty lamps and early candlesticks. The other room's focal point is a large open hearth with a bake oven. Although the upstairs sleeping loft is not accessible to the public, children enjoy hearing about how Caleb and his family got up there considering that there are no stairs. (They went outside, perched a ladder on the upper window, climbed in and pulled the ladder in behind them.) In addition to the house, the tour includes a visit to an 1849 school built for the children of workers from the local textile mill. It houses the gift shop and museum office and features exhibits of archeological material from the Pusey House excavation. A display of mid-19th-century clothing and school artifacts such as old-fashioned slates and textbooks are also on view.

The guides are engaging and enjoy young audiences. They are pleased to arrange reserved school-group tours and activities appropriate to the age of the children.

Delaware County "Pick Your Own" Farms

☐ **Fairhope Orchards**
180 Middletown Road, Glenn Mills, PA, (215) 399-0569.

Crops:	Peaches, apples.
Season, Hours:	June through October. Call ahead for hours.
Directions:	Intersection of Routes 352 and 926.

☐ **Linvilla Orchards**
137 West Knowlton Road, Media, PA, (215) 876-7116.

Crops:	Strawberries, raspberries, peaches, Concord grapes.
Season, Hours:	Call ahead for crop reports and hours.
Directions:	From the intersection of Routes 1 and 352, travel south on Route 352 and take a right at the second traffic light.

☐ **John F. Stoki Farm**
144 Beaver Valley Road, Chadds Ford, PA, (215) 358-0274.

Crops:	Grapes.
Season, Hours:	August through October. Call ahead for hours.
Directions:	One-half mile west of the intersection of Routes 202 and 491.

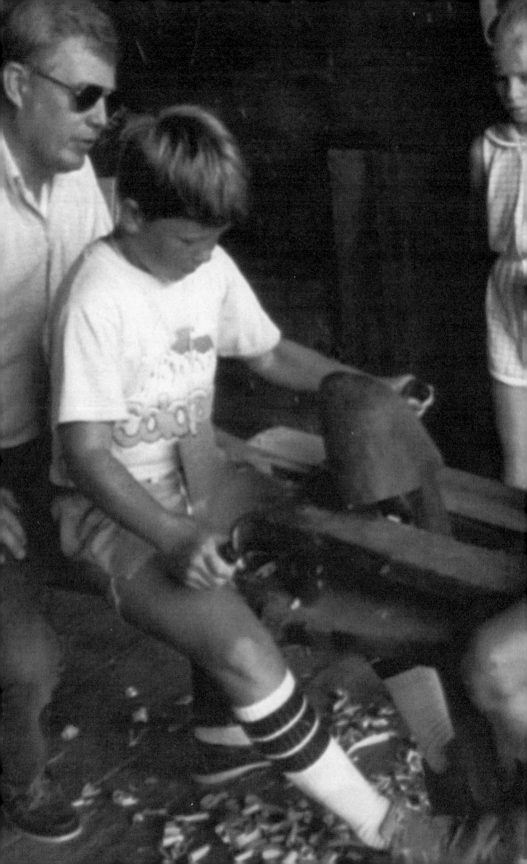

Montgomery County

Audubon Wildlife Sanctuary and Mill Grove
Pawlings and Audubon roads, Audubon, PA. (215) 666-5593. Grounds: Tuesday through Sunday, 7 a.m. to dusk; free. House: Tuesday through Saturday, 10 a.m. to 4 p.m.; Sunday, 1 to 4 p.m.; free.

John James Audubon, the famous artist, naturalist, and author, once lived on this 130-acre estate. The grounds, now converted to a wildlife sanctuary along with Mill Grove, the residence, are dedicated to the memory of this talented Frenchman, who lived on the property during the early 19th century. Many major works by Audubon, the first to portray birds and other wildlife in natural scale, color, and habitat, are housed in Mill Grove along with rooms of period furnishings, a recreated studio and taxidermy display, and Audubon memorabilia.

Outside in the sanctuary, families can stroll on miles of trails and observe birds in the nesting boxes and feeding stations, and in the specially planted shrubs and trees that have attracted over 175 species to the site. It's well worth a stop anytime, but the spring and fall migration periods are when the most unusual feathered friends appear.

Elmwood Park Zoo
Harding Boulevard, Norristown, PA. (215) 277-3825. Tuesday through Sunday, 10 a.m. to 4:30 p.m. Free.

This friendly, low-key municipal zoo is a best bet for very young animal observers. The furry, four-footed friends featured include bison,

Woodworking demonstration at the Peter Wentz Farmstead.

burros, cougars, elk, deer, foxes, gibbons, monkeys, prairie dogs, ponies, and raccoons. Waterfowl and birds of prey are also on view. During the summer months kids can have a hands-on experience in the petting zoo, where domestic chickens, goats, pigs, rabbits, and sheep share quarters with tame ferrets, raccoons, and an emu. Bring your stroller. Brown bag your lunch or buy it at the snack shack. Picnic tables are available.

Valley Forge National Historical Park

Route 23 and North Gulph Road, Valley Forge, PA. (215) 783-7700. Daily, 8:30 a.m. to 5 p.m.; until 6 p.m. in summer. Free.

If you visit only one Revolutionary War memorial with the kids, make it Valley Forge. This 3,000-acre park does a fabulous job of bringing the story of the struggle for American independence to life for visitors of all ages. The tour begins in the Visitors Center, where audiovisual presentations and exhibits, including George Washington's sleeping marquee, introduce you to the story of the 11,000 soldiers and officers encamped here

A costumed interpreter brings the Revolutionary War to life for a young tour group at Valley Forge National Historical Park.

during the brutal winter of 1777–1778. The sites on the tour include extensive remains and reconstructions of forts and earthworks, the Artillery Park, the headquarters of Generals Washington and Varnum, the Grand Parade, the Memorial Arch, the Memorial Chapel and Bell Tower, and the Museum of the Valley Forge Historical Society. Adults are charged a minimal admission to tour the interiors of Washington's and Varnum's headquarters and the museum.

You can explore the park by car on your own with the help of the Visitors Center map. Cassette tour tapes, designed to be used with the map, can be purchased at the Visitors Center. Bus tours are also available for a fee at certain times of the year. They are scheduled every half-hour from 9 a.m. to 4 p.m. during summer months and at 10 a.m. and 1 and 3 p.m. during the months of April, May, September, and October. Bicycles are available for rental during the summer months. Picnicking is permitted in designated areas of the park.

Special children's service include reserved group-tour programs on four different subjects. The tour subject titles are "The Life of the Soldier," "George Washington," "America in Rebellion," and "Small Things Forgotten," a look at archeology at Valley Forge. Each program includes a park tour.

Young visitors get a feel for the life of a Continental soldier at Valley Forge National Historical Park.

Peter Wentz Farmstead

Routes 73 and 363, Worcester, PA. (215) 584-5104. Tuesday through Saturday, 10 a.m. to 4 p.m.; Sunday, 1 to 4 p.m. Free.

Built in 1758, this farmstead incorporates the Georgian style so popular with Philadelphia's early English gentry, with elements of German construction, reflecting the traditions of its original owner, farmer Peter Wentz. It is here that George Washington planned the Battle of Germantown. The tour begins at the reception center where an audiovisual orientation can be viewed. A costumed guide accompanies visitors through the authentically furnished farmhouse, garden, and barn and pasture, where there are horses, cows, chicken, geese, and sheep. The guides are tuned in to young visitors. They make every effort to relate the story of the Wentz family and their life on the farm at a level youngsters can understand.

There's a bonus if you make your family visit to the farm on Saturday afternoon. Kids will enjoy the live period-crafts demonstrations and activities, including spinning, quilting, basket making, weaving, candle making, embroidery, theorem painting, and fireplace cooking and baking. Special children's services include reserved group tours that are individually tailored to the age group planning to visit.

Willow Grove Naval Air Station

Route 611, Horsham, PA. (215) 443-1776. By reservation only, April through October, 10 a.m. Free.

Your junior birdmen won't get up in the air here, but they'll learn a lot about flight and the operation of a naval air station. You'll tour a military aircraft if one is available and see how jump equipment is precisely packed in the parachute loft. In the fire station, you'll view the base's special aircraft fire-fighting equipment. A look at the base's collection of World War II–era planes is also part of the tour. When you call ahead to make your tour plans, ask about reservations for the reasonably priced lunches offered in the base dining room. Dining with the men and women in blue adds to the whole experience.

Montgomery County "Pick Your Own" Farms

☐ Appleville Orchards
133 Cressman Road, Telford, PA, (215) 723-6516.

Crops:	Strawberries, apples, blackberries.
Season, Hours:	June through November. Call ahead for hours.
Directions:	Two miles west of Harleysville on Route 63.

☐ F. W. McConnell Farm
Woxall, PA, (215) 234-4370.

Crops:	Strawberries, apples.
Season, Hours:	June through November. Call ahead for hours.
Directions:	Off Hendricks Station Road at Tabor Methodist Church (.75 mile from Route 63 at Sumneytown and 4 miles from Harleysville).

☐ Thomas Fruit Stand
Layfield Road, Pennsburg, PA, (215) 679-7701.

Crops:	Strawberries.
Season, Hours:	Late May through June. Call ahead for hours.
Directions:	Route 663, 3 miles south of Pennsburg.

Philadelphia County

Center City/Fairmount Park

Academy of Natural Sciences
19th Street and Benjamin Franklin Parkway, Philadelphia, PA. (215) 299-1000. Monday through Friday, 10 a.m. to 4 p.m.; Saturday and Sunday, 10 a.m. to 5 p.m. Children 3 to 12, $2.50; children under 3, free; adults, $4.50.

If your kids are fans of Tyrannosaurus Rex and his prehistoric buddies, don't miss visiting the Academy of Natural Sciences, one of the world's oldest natural history institutions. "Discovering Dinosaurs," a $2.5 million permanent exhibit, features over a dozen dinosaur specimens. Interactive stations allow visitors to seek out a wide variety of dinosaur pictures, facts, and figures on a visitor-directed video disk system. There is a scale that compares human and dinosaur body weights, a "strata wall" with drawers holding fossils from different geological periods, a "jaws" station where the lower facial bones of a dinosaur can be manipulated, a place to dig for fossils, and a large cast dinosaur footprint to step into. There is also a multimedia show on the scientific discovery of dinosaurs.

Another kid-pleasing exhibit is "Outside-In," a mini nature center designed especially for children under the age of 12. Natural wonders such as a live beehive, a fossil cave, an insect zoo, a sand dune, a miniature waterfall, and aquariums are explored by young visitors, with museum naturalists on hand to encourage discovery and offer impromptu lessons with the

A parent and child rest their bones in the shadow of a dinosaur skeleton at the Academy of Natural Sciences.

77

live animals they urge youngsters to touch. Other permanent museum of-
ferings include exhibits on gems and minerals, U.S. and world wildlife
specimens in natural habitats, Egyptian mummies, and daily ecology shows
in the museum auditorium, which are enhanced by the use of live animals.

Lunch at the museum, including sandwiches, beverages, and desserts, is
dispensed from vending machines. Children will enjoy a stop in the museum shop. It features books, jewelry, seashells, toys, and souvenirs that relate to the academy collections.

The academy has an expansive array of open and reserved children's
programs. "Back Porch Specials," two-hour non-reserved programs offered
once a month on Sundays, cover a given natural history subject through
the use of performers, storytellers, and hands-on arts and craft exercises.
Reserved school and camp tours, tailor-made to fit the age and size of a
children's group, can be arranged. Reserved Saturday and summer classes
offer young science enthusiasts in-depth exposure to specific areas of natural history. The academy staff also conducts outreach programs, bringing
live animals, demonstrations, slide shows, and films to young audiences
throughout the Delaware Valley. In addition, the academy teaches teachers
through workshops that aid educators in presenting contemporary science
concepts in the classroom.

*Children meet prehistoric pals at
"Discovering Dinosaurs," a permanent
exhibit at the Academy of Natural
Sciences.*

City Hall
Broad and Market streets, Philadelphia, PA. (215) 686-1776. Weekdays, 9 a.m. to 4:30 p.m. Free.

A statue of Philadelphia's founder, William Penn, is perched on the top layer of this wedding cake of a building, the largest city hall in the United States. Your family will enjoy the view that Penn has in City Hall Tower. Take the elevator along the north wall of the building to the seventh floor and follow the red lines to the elevator tower. When you come back down, visit the building's courtyard. It features city maps and plaques on the history of the city.

Franklin Institute
20th Street and Benjamin Franklin Parkway, Philadelphia, PA. (215) 448-1200. Monday through Saturday, 10 a.m. to 5 p.m.; Sunday, noon to 5 p.m. Children 4 to 12, $3.50; children under 4, free; adults, $4.50.

The ultimate "hands-on" museum, the Franklin Institute concentrates on letting visitors of all ages learn by doing. The aviation exhibit includes an Air Force jet trainer, models, films, flight simulators, and other hands-on devices that allow visitors to experiment with flight forces such as lift and thrust. An open wind tunnel tests the drag and lift of certain aircraft designs. The evolution of flight is illustrated in models, a film, and in a collection of Wright Brothers' artifacts that includes their Model B Flyer, suspended from the ceiling. In the Train Room, visitors can board a Baldwin locomotive for a 24-foot round-trip ride and view the wood-burning Pioneer, an engine that served the Cumberland Valley Railroad System until 1880. Model train exhibits show how the railway system shaped the modern transportation industry. In a video disk program, visitors view different trains in action.

A walk-through human heart illustrates blood circulation at the bioscience exhibit. You can also uncover the mysteries of DNA by building your own double helix with wooden puzzle pieces or lighting up different parts of an 18-foot model to see how genetic coding works.

The interactive video disks in the astronomy exhibit show time lapse sequences of solar flares, bringing life to a display that also includes a 30-foot layout of the planets and the sun, a 1699 hammered celestial globe, and a collection of ancient and modern telescopes. Solar system facts and figures are learned at astronomy computer stations. Visitors get a new perspective on the sun, moon, and planets when they view them through the powerful

A young visitor sees a fish from the inside out with the aid of an ultrasound machine at the Franklin Institute's Bioscience Exhibit.

telescopes of the institute's observatory. The institute's Fels Planetarium, the second oldest in the country, offers stargazers an unparalleled local resource. Two major public shows, on topics ranging from the history of astronomy to UFOs and black holes, are offered each year along with seasonal constellation programs and a traditional Christmas presentation.

"The Changing Earth," a two-level exhibit, explores the forces that shape the earth, with interactive devices and text. A stream table demonstrates the process of erosion. A rock wall shows different types and ages of rocks. A volcano made of plaster illustrates how eruptions occur. A weather station demonstration shows how radar and satellites are used to predict the weather.

An exhibit on communications explores the past, present, and future of communications technology with interactive devices and equipment displays. You can whisper a message into an oversized dish and have it heard across the room or send a written note flying across the ceiling in a pneumatic tube. Learn how television works and how programs and special effects are created. Step back into time and discover what went on in a colonial print shop, and how paper was made.

The electricity and electronics exhibit begins with static electricity demonstrations that will literally make your hair stand on end. You can learn how to tap out a message in Morse code and observe the push and pull of magnetic forces. In recreated turn-of-the-century storefronts, view what were then new time- and labor-saving electric devices: irons, toasters, and sewing machines. Turn the dial on an authentic 1930s radio and listen to Jack Benny, the Mills Brothers, and a "live" report on the crash of the *Hindenburg*. Electricity's modern age is represented by home computer displays, a visitor-operated remote television camera, and a music synthesizer that allows you to create music electronically.

Mechanics Hall is a physics resource room filled with hands-on equipment that teaches concepts such as energy, leverage, collision, momentum, and gravity. Computer terminals challenge visitors with a series of increasingly difficult physics experiments and problems.

Shipbuilding is the subject of another major exhibit at the institute. Ship plans, navigation instruments, ship models, and historical photos are complemented by the exhibit's hands-on and interactive components. A wave maker illustrates how a ship's design affects its speed in the water. Visitors see how a paddlewheel works and why an iron ship floats. Ancient maritime records and ship logs that detail mutinies, pirate raids, and typhoons

A youngster tries a hand at the ellipsograph, part of the Franklin Institute's Mathematics Exhibit.

were used to form the database for the exhibit's computer game, Sea Trader. Players choose a ship, cargo, and trade route that will make or break their fortune.

In the Science Arcade the principles of geometry, mathematics, and momentum are reinforced as visitors play computer games. Golf Classic requires a player to calculate the angle and distance needed for each shot on a golf course. Rocket Mail challenges the participant to guess the angle of ascent and the fuel needed to launch a rocket over a mountaintop to reach a target.

Before you leave, don't forget to give Old Ben his due. His statue and the country's largest collection of Franklin artifacts are housed in the institute's massive domed marble hall, designated by Congress in 1972 as the national memorial to its most famous native-born scientist and diplomat.

Ground was recently broken for a 90,000-square-foot addition: the Futures Center and Omniverse Theater. The center will feature exhibits that explore the future worlds of space, earth, energy, health, chemistry, and computers. The Omniverse Theater will be designed to project special motion picture film onto a domed screen that completely surrounds an audience of 300 people. Stay tuned, but don't wait for the completion of the new addition to plan a visit. The Franklin Institute is already a Delaware Valley "must visit" family destination. Multiple visits are recommended just to cover what is currently on display.

Fast food lunches are available at the institute. Other options are packing a lunch to eat outside or grabbing a hot dog and soda from one of the many food cart vendors around the entrance.

Nearly every subject covered in the institute's exhibits can be explored in a reserved children's group program conducted on the premises or in the classroom. A seasonal schedule of such programs is offered annually. All arrangements are made through the school group coordinator.

Philadelphia Museum of Art

26th Street and Benjamin Franklin Parkway. (215) 763-8100. Tuesday through Sunday, 10 a.m. to 5 p.m. Children 18 and under, $2; adults, $4. Free on Sunday from 10 a.m. to 1 p.m.

This extraordinary art museum, the third largest in the country, has vast and varied holdings of over 300,000 works in 200 galleries. If you've seen the film *Rocky*, you'll know the building from the outside. The underdog fighter ascended the museum's mountainous outdoor staircase while training for his big match. Inside, the museum's art treasures represent nearly

Children enjoy the participatory exhibits at the Franklin Institute, the ultimate "hands-on" museum.

every period of recorded history. There are French impressionist paintings, medieval weapons, armor and tapestries, the Arensberg Collection of contemporary art, French and Italian Renaissance works, examples of American crafts, decorative and fine arts, and architectural elements that include a Japanese teahouse, a Chinese palace hall, an early French cloister, and an ancient Indian temple. National and international touring exhibits are also standard fare at the museum.

How do you make the most of a family visit? Take a one-hour guided museum-highlights tour. They're offered Tuesday through Sunday on the hour from 11 a.m. to 3 p.m. You can get an overview and return to points of interest later the same day, or on another visit.

The large and well-stocked museum store is worth a stop. Lunch and snacks are available in the cafeteria, open weekdays 10 a.m. to 3:30 p.m. and weekends 11 a.m. to 3:45 p.m.

After your introductory tour, you'll want to come back for the museum's non-reserved Sunday family programs. In "Gallery Games," families engage in specially prepared activities that relate to the works in one of the galleries. A theme or subject meaningful to young people is explored through selected works in various galleries in "Family Tour." "Tales and Treasures" includes a discussion of the myths, fables, tall tales, or true stories that re-

Drawing classes are one of many children's activities offered at the Philadelphia Museum of Art.

late to certain gallery objects, along with a hands-on studio art project. Little ones are read a story and asked to associate the story's subject with what they see on the walls of the museum in "Early Bird Read and Look."

The museum also offers a great selection of children's general and special-subject reserved group tours scheduled by the education department. In addition, kids can register for various studio art classes.

Philadelphia Zoo
34th Street and Girard Avenue, Philadelphia, PA. (215) 243-1100. Daily, 9:30 a.m. to 5 p.m. Children 2 to 11, $3; children under 2, free; adults, $4.

Over 1,600 mammals, birds, and reptiles reside on the premises of the country's oldest zoo, located on the grounds of the 8,700-acre Fairmount Park, the world's largest municipal green space. In the "World of Primates," visitors observe their ancestral cousins in a one-acre jungle habitat. Gibbons, gorillas, lemurs, monkeys, and orangutangs make their home here.

**Nose to nose with a llama at the
Philadelphia Zoo**

"Bear Country" features bruins of all sizes and varieties. In the Reptile House, automated thunderstorms keep the slithering residents happy but have little effect on the neighboring fish population. The Bird House is the communal nest of many species of feathered friends. Antelope, giraffes, and zebras coexist in the zoo's African Plains exhibit. Check the zoo's posted feeding schedules. Chow time is a great opportunity to see lions, tigers, and elephants in action.

Other special features are Tree House, a new exhibit that encourages visitors to climb, crawl, swing, and discover their own animal magnetism; the warm-weather petting zoo; and the Monorail Safari, a 20-minute zoo tour aboard a small, sleek train, offered from April through November.

There are designated picnic areas and numerous food concession stands. The zoo's Impala Cafe offers lunches and snacks indoors or out.

Please Touch Museum

210 North 21st Street, Philadelphia, PA. (215) 963-0667. Tuesday through Sunday, 10 a.m. to 4:30 p.m. $3.50 per person.

If you have little ones, the Please Touch Museum is the place to visit. Opened in 1976, it is the country's first museum for children under the age of seven. Ongoing exhibits include "You Can Be," where children use costumes, puppets, and masks to play the role of their choice; "Animals as Pets," which highlights small live critters to watch and pet; "Calliope," an exhibit about musical sounds; "Circus," where kids can choose roles as human or animal performers under the big top; "Native American Corner," where kids sit inside an authentic wigwam and learn how to grind corn; and the "Office," "Grocery Store," and "Health Care Center," which offer access to the hands-on activities that occur in these work environments. In the "Tot Spot," very young children can crawl, climb, and explore in safety. The museum's Childlife Center features two giant folk-art toys, hands-on activities, and exhibits that relate to the history of childhood in the Delaware Valley. The museum also sponsors two changing exhibits each year.

A brown bag lunch can be eaten in the museum's Tortoise Lounge or outside in one of the nearby parks. Another recommended stop is the museum store, full of toys, games, crafts, and an excellent selection of children's books.

Special children's services are numerous. There are films or performances every Saturday and Sunday during the summer at 11 a.m. and 2 p.m. Reserved 1½-hour Saturday workshops on arts and science topics are also scheduled. The museum will make arrangements for birthday parties. Reserved group tours are available, as are traveling trunk programs on a variety of subjects. The museum also sponsors reserved workshops for parents and child educators.

East Philadelphia (Historic District)

Afro-American Historical and Cultural Museum
Seventh and Arch streets, Philadelphia, PA. (215) 574-0380. Tuesday through Saturday, 10 a.m. to 5 p.m.; Sunday, noon to 6 p.m. Children under 12, free; adults, $1.50.

Opened as part of the Bicentennial Celebration in 1976, this museum is the first and largest institution devoted to the black American experience. In the museum's multilevel galleries, there are changing art and history exhibits that depict Afro-American lifestyles and cultural contributions in the region, state, and nation. African jewelry, clothing, and artifacts along with a variety of books are available in the museum store. Special reserved children's group tours and study programs on topics such as Afro-American music are available.

Betsy Ross House
239 Arch Street, Philadelphia, PA. (215) 627-5343. Daily, 9 a.m. to 5 p.m. Free.

Every heart beats true for the red, white, and blue and so will yours when you visit the lovely little home of America's most famous seamstress. Outside you'll see a replica of the flag Betsy stitched. Inside you'll see period furnishings and artifacts that tell the story of this busy 18th-century wife, mother, homemaker, career woman, and patriot.

Elfreth's Alley Museum
126 Elfreth's Alley (Second Street between Arch and Race streets). (215) 547-0560. Daily, 10 a.m. to 4 p.m. Free.

Elfreth's Alley is America's oldest continuously occupied residential street. Its charming little houses are typical working-class dwellings of the early 18th century. At Number 126, the Elfreth's Alley Museum, visitors can see how a tradesman and his family might have lived in the two downstairs rooms, decorated with period furnishings. Upstairs you can view photographs of the interiors of other Elfreth's Alley homes that are privately owned. Tours of the entire neighborhood are offered once a year on the first Sunday in June from noon to 5 p.m.

Fireman's Hall
Second and Quarry Streets, Philadelphia, PA. (215) 923-1438. Tuesday through Saturday, 9 a.m. to 5 p.m. Free.

Kids will love following the history of fire fighting from colonial days to the recent past at this restored 1903 firehouse. Fire-fighting memorabilia, films, and gear including uniforms, hand tools, ladders, leather buckets, jump nets, and hoses are on view. Hand pumpers and steamers are out in the open to see and touch. Manually powered, horse-drawn, and motorized rolling stock is displayed. You can get behind the wheel of a fireboat, visit the recreated quarters of the chief and his firemen, and watch as a mannequin slides down the brass pole. The tour is self-guided, but a friendly fire fighter is usually on hand to answer questions and offer information.

Independence National Historical Park

Known as America's most historic square mile, the park encompasses over 36 historic buildings and sites. It is here that Americans cast off their colonial yoke, planned the war that would liberate them, and instituted a new government to preserve and nourish their hard-won freedom. At the risk of sounding sentimental, I regard a visit to the park as the ultimate "roots" experience for every American family, no matter who they are or how they or their ancestors entered the country. Although each and every park location has a special significance, I've focused only on those that are particularly meaningful to children. Adults may wish to investigate the other sites by themselves.

□ Visitors Center
Third and Chestnut streets, Philadelphia, PA. (215) 597-8974. Daily, 9 a.m. to 5 p.m. Free.

I momentarily abandoned alphabetizing and listed the Visitors Center first, hoping that you'll stop here before proceeding through the park. The park rangers and volunteers do a magnificent job of orienting the troops and suggesting tour sites and routes based on the size and age of those in your party. Don't leave before you watch *Independence,* a half-hour film by John Huston that beautifully depicts the historic events that took place in the environs of the park. Check out the building's belltower. It houses the Bicentennial Bell, a 200th birthday gift from the British government to the people of the United States to show that there are no hard feelings It was cast at London's White Chapel Bell Foundry, the same company that made the Liberty Bell in 1751. It rings every day at 11 a.m. and 3 p.m. A stop at the center's gift shop is warranted. Here you'll find excellent guidebooks, replicas of the Declaration of Independence and Constitution, color slides, and mementos of park buildings.

☐ **Army Navy Museum**
Chestnut Street between Third and Fourth streets, Philadelphia, PA. (215) 597-8974. Daily, 9 a.m. to 5 p.m. Free.

The focus inside this recreated 18th-century residence is the military history of America from the time of the Revolutionary War to the beginning of the 19th century. Regimental uniforms, flags, weapons, and battle dioramas and ship models make up the exhibits. Visitors can also play look-out on the simulated gun deck of an early frigate.

☐ **Carpenter's Hall**
320 Chestnut Street, Philadelphia, PA. (215) 925-0167. Tuesday through Sunday, 10 a.m. to 4 p.m. Free.

Carpenter's Hall was built in 1770 by a craftsmen's guild to help its members improve their skills in building and architecture and to aid their families in times of need. In September of 1774, the First Continental Congress met here to air their grievances against King George III. During the Revolutionary War the hall served as an arsenal and hospital for the Continental forces. In 1791, the First Bank of the United States was headquartered here before moving to its Third Street location later in the decade. Early documents, tools, and furnishings used by the guild's 18th-century builders and woodcrafters are displayed along with an architect's model of the building and information that describes the techniques and materials used in its construction.

☐ **Christ Church**
Second and Market streets, Philadelphia, PA. (215) 922-1695. Monday through Saturday, 9 a.m. to 5 p.m.; Sunday, 1 to 5 p.m. Free.

Where did leading Episcopalian patriots and loyalists worship in 18th-century Philadelphia? Right here. The present building dates back to the early 1700s, but the church was founded in 1695. This is where Washington, Franklin, Betsy Ross, and Robert Morris attended Sunday services. Guides will show you their pews and a stained-glass window that portrays them.

☐ **Christ Church Burial Ground**
Fifth and Arch streets, Philadelphia, PA. (215) 922-1695.
April through October, 9 a.m. to 4:30 p.m. Free.

This is where Benjamin Franklin, his wife and two children rest in peace along with seven other signers of the Declaration of Independence. Local lore has it that a penny pitched on Old Ben's grave will bring good luck.

☐ **Franklin Court**
314 to 322 Market Street, Philadelphia, PA. (215) 597-2760 or 597-2761.
Daily, 9 a.m. to 5 p.m. Free.

This and the Liberty Bell will be the kids' favorite stop in the park. The Franklin Court complex is a lively and likable spot for an introduction to America's Renaissance man, Benjamin Franklin. On the plot where Ben's house once stood is a steel "ghost structure" that outlines the contours of his Georgian residence, demolished only 20 years after his death. Underneath is an unbelievable underground museum. Its Hall of Mirrors shows the many facets of the man. At the Franklin Exchange, you can place a telephone call to a number of prominent American historical and cultural figures like Mark Twain or Harry Truman and hear their opinions of Ben. "Franklin on the World Stage," a 10-minute mechanized puppet show, relives some of Ben's best moments including his appearance at the British House of Commons, his service as envoy to France, and his speech to the Constitutional Convention. An 18-minute film, *Portrait of a Family,* gives viewers a look into the relationships Ben had with his wife and two children.

Other Franklin Court attractions are housed in five stately dwellings adjacent to the ghost structure. In these buildings, three of which were planned and built by Franklin, you can see the artifacts that were found during archeological digs on the Franklin property, visit a recreated print shop, and take your postcards and letters to the B. Free Franklin Post Office, where U.S. postal workers, dressed in colonial costumes, hand cancel all mail.

□ **Independence Hall**
Chestnut Street between Fifth and Sixth streets, Philadelphia, PA. (215) 627-1776. Daily, 9 a.m. to 5 p.m. Free.

The only way you can see this building is by guided tour. Tours originate in the East Wing. What you'll see is truly worth waiting for. Originally the State House of colonial Pennsylvania, the building became the meetingplace for the Second Continental Congress. It was in the hall's assembly room that Washington was appointed commander in chief of the Continental Army in 1775. It is where the Declaration of Independence was adopted on July 4, 1776, and where the U. S. Constitution was written in 1787. Although most of the original furnishings were destroyed when the British occupied Philadelphia during the Revolutionary War, a few original objects remain. They include Washington's Chippendale chair with sunburst carving and the silver inkwell delegates used to sign the Declaration of Independence and the Constitution.

□ **Liberty Bell Pavilion**
Independence Mall, Market Street between Fifth and Sixth streets, Philadelphia, PA. (215) 597-8974. Open 24 hours daily. Free.

Although many associate the Liberty Bell with the American Revolution, it was cast to celebrate a smaller but important victory for freedom. It was created to commemorate the 50th anniversary of the Pennsylvania Charter of Privileges, the democratic constitution that a forward-thinking William Penn granted his colony in 1701.

It arrived in Philadelphia from London's White Chapel Bell Foundry in 1752 and was cracked during a trial ring. After being recast by city workmen John Pass and John Stow, it was hung in the belltower of the State House, now Independence Hall. Tradition has it that the bell's next crack occurred while it tolled during Chief Justice John Marshall's funeral in 1835. The last time the bell was rung was during Washington's birthday celebration in 1846. The 2,000-pound bell's inscription, "Proclaim Lib-

*Independence Hall, Independence
National Historical Park*

The Liberty Bell, Independence Hall,
Independence National Historical Park

erty," inspired early-19th-century abolitionists, who took the bell as their symbol and gave it the name that sticks today.

As a kick-off to the national Bicentennial celebration in 1976, the bell was moved from Independence Hall to its new home in the glass pavilion just after midnight on New Year's Day. Park interpreters are on hand daily from 9 a.m. to 5 p.m. to chat with visitors, who can see and touch the bell. At other times, you can view the bell through the glass and listen to its history by using one of the outside audio stations.

☐ **Second Bank of the United States**
*420 Chestnut Street, Philadelphia, PA. (215) 597-9579. Daily, 9 a.m. to
5 p.m. Free.*

While the importance of this early-19th-century building as an example of
Greek Revival architecture may be lost on the kiddos, they'll enjoy what's
inside. Nearly 200 portraits and sculptures of 18th-century leaders such as
Washington, Jefferson, Franklin, Madison, and Lafayette are exhibited, giv-
ing visitors a chance to meet early America's movers and shakers face to
face.

National Museum of American Jewish History
*55 North Fifth Street, Philadelphia, PA. (215) 923-3811. Monday through
Thursday, 10 a.m. to 5 p.m.; Sunday, noon to 5 p.m. Children, $1.25; adults,
$1.75.*

The museum's permanent exhibit details the experience of Jews in this
country from before the time of William Penn to the present through artifacts and text. Two smaller exhibit spaces feature changing exhibits. The
museum offers unreserved family events and prescheduled school and
camp group programs for children. For young children there is a puppet
show of characters from American Jewish history that depicts traditional
Jewish values, and "My Grandmother's Trunk," a look at artifacts that de-
fine Jewish-American life in the last century. "Justice for All," an interactive
program that details the major court decisions made by three Jewish Su-
preme Court justices, is available for older children. All programs can be
presented at the museum or in the classroom.

Penn's Landing

In 1682 William Penn arrived here in the *Welcome* and proceeded to found
the town whose name means "brotherly love" in Greek. In more recent history, time-ravaged piers and broken-down buildings were cleared to create
what Philadelphians consider to be the city's newest jewel. Penn's Landing,
encompassing about six blocks of riverfront property along the Delaware
from Market to South streets, is land-use planning at its best. There are
marinas, water-side walkways, historic ships, restaurants, and a theater for
open-air performances. Maritime information panels exhibited along the

water acquaint visitors with the ships commonly seen on the river and what their flags signify. It's a great place to observe the action on the river, eat a picnic lunch, or attend one of the many city concerts scheduled throughout the year. Now for the places to visit at Penn's Landing.

☐ **Gazela of Philadelphia**
The Delaware River at Dock Street, Philadelphia, PA. (215) 923-9030. Weekends, 12:30 to 5:30 p.m. Suggested donation: $1 per person.

This 180-foot wooden ship is the world's oldest and largest sailing vessel in operable condition. Formerly one of a fleet of Portuguese fishing ships, she now functions as a live exhibit and training facility. Visitors can tour the decks, living quarters, and hold. Call ahead to be sure the *Gazela's* in port. She's often out stealing the show in tall-ship exhibitions along the eastern seaboard.

☐ **U.S.S. *Becuna*, U.S.S. *Olympia***
The Delaware River at Spruce Street, Philadelphia, PA. (215) 922-1898. Daily, 10 a.m. to 4:30 p.m. Children, $1.50; adults, $3.

One ticket admits visitors to both ships. The *Becuna,* a World War II submarine that served in the South Pacific and Atlantic, was later used as a training vessel. The *Olympia,* a steel steam-powered battleship, is the last survivor of the Spanish American War. In 1921, she transported the Unknown Soldier back from France for his burial in Arlington National Cemetery. Visitors can tour her decks, cabin, and berths and view exhibits of naval artillery, uniforms, and memorabilia from the Spanish-American War.

☐ ***Moshulu* Maritime Exhibit**
The Delaware River at Chestnut Street, Philadelphia, PA. (215) 925-3237. Monday through Saturday, 11 a.m. to 6 p.m.; Sunday, 1 to 6 p.m. Free.

The world's largest steel sailing ship still afloat, the *Moshulu,* built in 1904, is now a restaurant. It's 400 feet long and as tall as a ten-story building. Aside from food, it also features a museum of photographs, artifacts, and memorabilia that tell of her former exploits as a cargo ship transporting coal, lumber, and grain to ports around the world.

☐ **Workshop on the Water**
Delaware River at Dock Street, Philadelphia, PA. (215) 925-7589. May through September: Wednesday through Sunday, 9:30 a.m. to 4:30 p.m. Donation requested.

At one end of this 110-foot barge are authentic examples of small sailing boats that were used on the Delaware over the last three centuries. On the other end is a workshop where replicas of these small vessels are under construction. The public can watch as workshop participants practice their boat-building skills, or participate themselves by calling ahead to register for a workshop.

Philadelphia Maritime Museum
321 Chestnut Street, Philadelphia, PA. (215) 925-5439. Monday through Saturday, 10 a.m. to 5 p.m.; Sunday, 1 to 5 p.m. Donation requested.

The focus of this museum is maritime history in general and the port of Philadelphia in specific. In the main gallery on the first floor, handsome contemporary exhibits of ship models, naval weaponry, navigational instruments, scrimshaw, harpoons, naval blueprints, and a collection of miniature silver ships depict the regional history of life on the water. Also featured is an exhibit of artifacts from the *Titanic*. Changing and loaned exhibits are located in second-floor galleries. In the museum's open storage section on the third floor, visitors can see restorations in progress and view maritime artifacts and materials stored for use in future museum presentations.
    The museum offers children a variety of reserved group programs, among them "Maritime Adventure," "Life on a Frigate," "Privateers of the American Revolution," "Whales and Whalers," "Philadelphia Colonial Merchants," and "Ships: Fact and Fancy." Each includes a museum tour and hands-on activities.

Old Saint Joseph's Church
Fourth and Walnut streets, Philadelphia, PA. (215) 923-1733. Daily, 6:30 a.m. to 6 p.m. Free.

This is Philadelphia's oldest Roman Catholic congregation. The present building was completed in 1838, over a century after the parish was founded in 1733. When Catholicism was outlawed in England and many of the colonies, St. Joseph's was one of few places along the eastern seaboard where Masses were celebrated.

United States Mint

Fifth and Arch streets, Philadelphia, PA. (215) 597-7350. April through December: Monday through Saturday, 9 a.m. to 4:30 p.m. January through March: Weekdays only. Free.

Have your kids ever wondered where their allowance comes from? Chances are the coins they spend on candy or hoard in their piggy banks were made right here at the country's largest mint. Take the self-guided audio-visual tour and see how pennies, nickels, dimes, and quarters are cast, pressed, inspected, and counted. The manufacturing process can be viewed from an enclosed observation gallery.

South Philadelphia/Queen Village

American-Swedish Historical Museum

1900 Pattison Avenue, Philadelphia, PA. (215) 389-1776. Tuesday through Friday, 10 a.m. to 4 p.m.; Saturday, noon to 4 p.m. Children under 12, free; adults, $1.50.

In Roosevelt Park, on the site of what was part of the 17th-century colony of New Sweden, stands this museum, a recreated Swedish manor house. Inside, exhibits celebrate the cultural, social, and artistic contributions of early Swedish settlers and their American-born descendants. Kids will enjoy the pioneer craft and folk art displays that include toys and a large collection of dolls in native costumes.

Mummers Museum

Second Street and Washington Avenue, Philadelphia, PA. (215) 336-3050. Tuesday through Saturday, 9:30 a.m. to 5 p.m.; Sunday, noon to 5 p.m. Children under 12, 75¢; adults, $1.50.

What's 2.55 miles long, 69 feet wide, 12 feet high, and covered with feathers? Philadelphia's New Year's Day Mummers Parade, of course. From whence did the Mummers come? In merry old England costumed villager families often reenacted traditional pantomime plays and legends for each other at Christmas. Early English settlers in Philadelphia brought this tradition with them. With succeeding generations the pageantry became more elaborate and music was added. The result of this evolution is what marches down Broad Street on the first day of the year.

At the museum, visitors get a quick indoctrination to Mummerdom. You'll find out how clubs are organized, how club parade themes are selected, how costumes are constructed and their weight and cost. At audiovisual exhibits, you can compose your own string-band music and watch films of performers in past parades. You won't leave without learning how to do the Mummer's strut.

Old Fort Mifflin

Fort Mifflin Road and the Delaware River, Philadelphia, PA. (215) 365-9781. March through December: Weekends, noon to 5 p.m. Children, 25¢; adults, 50¢.

The building of Fort Mifflin was begun at the direction of the British in 1772. It was completed by Continental forces in 1776 under the watchful eye of Benjamin Franklin. In 1777, 400 Revolutionary soldiers attacked a fleet of 250 British ships and 2,000 troops on their way up the river. The lives of 250 colonial fighting men were lost. The fort is a tribute to their memory. On view are authentic and reproduction weapons and vehicles of the period, an arsenal, officer's and soldier's quarters, a blacksmith shop, and exhibits of fort artifacts and memorabilia. Visit on Sunday, and you're likely to catch volunteers engaged in battle reenactments and other 18th-century military activities. Picnicking is permitted and soda machines are available.

Old Swedes' Church (Gloria Dei)

Swanson and Christian streets, Philadelphia, PA. (215) 389-1513. Daily, 9 a.m. to 5 p.m. Free.

Built in 1700, Old Swedes' Church is one of Pennsylvania's oldest buildings. Affiliated with the Episcopal Church in 1845, the congregation began worship in 1646 in a log cabin. Inside, notice the maritime models hanging

An eye-popping Mummer's costume from
the Mummer's Museum.

from the ceiling. They are replicas of the ships that brought the first Swedish settlers to America. A 17th-century bible that belonged to Sweden's Queen Christina is also displayed.

Tinicum National Environmental Center
86th Street and Lindbergh Boulevard, Philadelphia, PA. (215) 365-3118. Daily, 8 a.m. until sunset; Visitors Center, 8:30 to 4 p.m. Free.

Operated by the U.S. Fish and Wildlife Service, Tinicum is the last remaining freshwater tidal marsh in Pennsylvania. Here over 280 bird species live or visit during seasonal migrations. Muskrats, rabbits, snakes, turtles, and weasels are permanent residents. Bring your binoculars and camera to make the most of the center's observation platform and photography blind, both stops on the self-guided walking tour of this 1,200-acre preserve. Weekly guided nature walks that focus on special subjects are offered Saturday and Sunday mornings at 9 a.m. Call ahead for the subject de jour. Wear comfy shoes and pack a picnic.

West Philadelphia

Institute of Contemporary Art
University of Pennsylvania, Myerson Hall, 34th and Walnut streets, Philadelphia, PA. (215) 898-7180. Daily, 10 a.m. to 5 p.m. Free.

The four changing exhibits presented by the institute every year feature individual contemporary artists, or emerging themes or schools of modern work. Although the institute is part of the University of Pennsylvania, its educational mission extends well beyond Penn students. Satuday and Sunday morning nonreserved children's workshops are scheduled with each new exhibit. They include a kiddie-oriented galley talk and a hands-on art activity. Call ahead for the workshop schedule.

University Museum

University of Pennsylvania, 33rd and Spruce streets, Philadelphia, PA. (215) 898-4000. Tuesday through Saturday, 10 a.m. to 4:30 p.m.; Sunday, 1 to 5 p.m. Children, $1.50; adults, $3. Free on Tuesday.

The traveling King Tut exhibit took the country by storm a few years back, sparking a renewed interest in past civilizations among American museum visitors of all ages. If your kids have an interest in the ancients, the University Museum is the place to be. The primitive art and artifacts from over 300 university-sponsored archeological digs are imaginatively displayed here along with other acquired relics. The sphinx and the 4,000-year-old mummies will fascinate any budding Egyptologists. Remnants of ancient Greek, Roman, Middle Eastern, African, and Polynesian cultures are also on view. South and Central America's past civilizations are discovered in exhibits of objects from the Aztec, Maya, and Inca tribes. The tools, weapons, and ceremonial artifacts of North America's earliest residents are also displayed.

Hot or cold lunches can be purchased for a reasonable price in the museum cafeteria. The main museum store has a unusual array of books, artifact reproductions, interesting jewelry and handicrafts. The Pyramid Shop for children carries a small but special selection of low-cost games, books, and mementos that relate to the collection.

The museum offers a number of reserved group subject tours for children. They are guided by a museum staff member or the classroom teacher, who receives orientation materials in advance of the visit.

Southern New Jersey

New Jersey, contrary to the opinion of many, is home to much more than the interstate highway between Philadelphia and New York or the tinsel and flash of Atlantic City. The history of its Swedish and English Quaker settlements along the Delaware River are a significant part of America's colonial past. Numerous battlefields, monuments, and museums reveal the important role New Jersey played during the Revolutionary War. Home to glass, iron, and machine manufacturing businesses for centuries, New Jersey's current contributions to the GNP are based on a proud and hard-working industrial heritage. The productive farms that stretch on for miles over the lower flatlands have earned for New Jersey the title Garden State. Its state parks and forests are living testaments to a state-wide love affair with open space and nature. Next time you're zooming up or down the turnpike on a family trip, pull off and visit one or two of the places listed in the following chapter. You'll see what you've been missing.

Ride 'em cowboy. A bull-riding event at Cowtown Rodeo.

Burlington County

Batsto Village and Wharton State Forest
Route 542, Hammonton, NJ. (609) 561-3262. **Village:** *June through August, daily, 10 a.m. to 6 p.m.; September through May, daily, 11 a.m. to 5 p.m. Free.* **Guided Tour:** *Children 6 to 11, 75¢; children under 6, free; adults, $1.50.* **Forest:** *Daily, dawn to dusk; free.*

Tucked in the Wharton State Forest, part of New Jersey's Pine Barren region, is Batsto Village, an early American bog ironworks famous during the Revolutionary War for its cast cannon and cannonballs. In the mid-19th century, lumber and glass were added to this self-sufficient village's product line. Today the village, built on the banks of the Batsto Lake and River, is owned by the state and open for public perusal.

A village tour begins at the Visitor Center. Here visitors view exhibits on the history of the Pine Barrens, the village, and its former industries. You can buy a ticket for a guided tour that includes the ironmaster's mansion, the carriage shed, the blacksmith shop, and the gristmill. Other village buildings and exhibits such as the ore boat, charcoal kiln, ice- and milk house, general store, post office, workers' cottages, corncrib, mule barn, horse barn, piggery, and threshing barn are opened for self-guided viewing at no charge. During summer weekends period crafts such as pottery, candle making, chair caning, weaving, and spinning are demonstrated on a sporadic basis by artisans who now live in what were the old worker's quarters. Stagecoach rides are another warm-weather activity offered for a minimal fee. Because of ongoing building restorations and staff shortages, you may find some of the facility closed at the time you visit. Even so, Batsto is a fascinating place to observe life as it was lived in an early industrial community.

Before or after your visit to the village, take advantage of some of the other facilities and activities offered in Wharton Forest Park. You can paddle the lake in a rented canoe, picnic, swim, fish, or hike on one of the nature trails. Playground equipment is also available. In the winter months ice fishing and ice skating are permitted.

Burlington County Historical Society
457 High Street, Burlington, NJ. (609) 386-4473. Monday through Thursday, 1 to 4 p.m.; Sunday, 2 to 4 p.m. Donation requested.

This active historical society has restored three interesting properties right next to each other. The James Fenimore Cooper House will be of interest to young readers who have enjoyed *The Last of the Mohicans* or *The Deerslayer,* two of Cooper's best-known books. This is the house where he was born in 1789. Exhibits include his dining implements, bedroom furnishings, and other memorabilia. Also on view are some possessions of Joseph Bonaparte's. He served as king of Spain but fled to New Jersey in 1817 after his brother, Napoleon, lost the Battle of Waterloo.

Next is the Aline Wolcott Museum. It was a print shop and now displays early tools, lighting equipment, and kitchen utensils along with changing exhibits that reflect the county's industries and handicrafts. Of particular interest to children are the 19th-century costume and doll collections.

The Capt. James Lawrence House is next. A naval officer during the War of 1812, Lawrence is famous for the line, "Don't give up the ship." Some of his personal belongings and papers are on view in the house along with changing period clothing and quilt exhibits.

Historic Burlington County Prison Museum
128 High Street, Mount Holly, NJ. (609) 265-5958. April through November: Wednesday and Saturday, 10 a.m. to noon and 1 to 4 p.m. Donation requested.

A visit to this little gem of a museum could motivate kids to be on their best behavior, for a little while at least. On the tour of this 1810 jailhouse, they'll see the men's and women's cells, the dining facilities and workrooms. The dungeon, the early equivalent of a solitary confinement cell, is said to be haunted by the ghost of a murderer who spent his last night within its confines. Also on view are materials on Robert Mills, who designed the prison. Appointed Federal Architect in 1936, Mills's later designs include the U.S. Treasury Department, the U.S. Patent and Post offices, and the National Monument in Washington.

Smithville Mansion
Route 38, Mount Holly, NJ. (609) 265-5068. April through November: Wednesday, 10 a.m. to 3 p.m.; Sunday, 1 to 4 p.m. Children, $1; adults, $1.50.

Formerly an early cotton milling town, this industrial community and stately owner's residence along the Rancocas Creek was purchased lock, stock, and barrel by New England industrialist Hezekiah Bradely Smith in 1865. Smith retooled factories to produce a wide variety of woodworking machinery, built a progressive new workers' community, and bought up acres of adjacent farmland to produce the foodstuffs needed by the growing town. In the 1880s H.B. Smith and Company entered the transportation market with the invention of the Star bicycle, a high-wheeler with a small guiding wheel in front to increase stability. The company later built a bicycle railway designed to improve transportation for an ever-increasing number of workers who were commuting to Smithville from nearby Mount Holly.

A tour of Smith's mansion reveals much about the heyday of self-made American industrialists. It begins in a building that was once used as a schoolhouse for workers' children. Here visitors view an 18-panel exhibit on the site that includes information on its early history, biographical details about Smith, and authentic Star bicycles and track from the bike railway. In the mansion itself, guides concentrate on the furnishings. The mansion annex, with its dining rooms, bowling alley, and card and billiard rooms, gives visitors a peek at how this powerful industrialist entertained equally powerful business associates and politicians. Also included is an amble through the home's adjacent formal gardens.

During the mansion's operating season, visitors are welcome to take a free self-guided walking tour of the other buildings that make up this industrial village. Guides are happy to provide walking tour maps. Special children's services include reserved group tours that are individually designed to appeal to the age group planning to visit.

Burlington County "Pick Your Own" Farms

□ Bud Wells Farm

Sooy Place Road, Vincentown, NJ, (609) 726-1116.

Crops:	Blueberries.
Season, Hours:	Mid-June to mid-August, daily from 8 a.m. to 5:30 p.m.
Directions:	Three miles east of Red Lion Circle on Route 70.

□ Creek Water Farm

East Landing Street, Lumberton, NJ, (609) 261-8782.

Crops:	Strawberries.
Season, Hours:	Mid-May to mid-June. Call ahead for hours.
Directions:	One mile east of Lumberton off Route 541.

□ Edward Wells Farm

Retreat Road, Vincentown, NJ, (609) 859-2662.

Crops:	Blueberries.
Season, Hours:	Mid-June to mid-August. Call ahead for hours.
Directions:	On Retreat Road, 3.5 miles east of State Highway 206.

□ Four Winds Farm

Medford Lakes Road, Tabernacle, NJ, (609) 268-9113.

Crops:	Blueberries, raspberries, blackberries, strawberries, pumpkins.
Season, Hours:	Mid-May through October, daily. Call ahead for hours.
Directions:	On Route 532, .5 mile east of Route 206.

□ Fred + III Farm

Pemberton-Juliustown Road, Pemberton, NJ, (609) 894-8822.

Crops:	Blueberries.
Season, Hours:	Mid-June to mid-August. Call ahead for hours.
Directions:	The farm is right on Route 663.

□ **Gladwill Farms**
Old Indian Mill Road, Tabernacle, NJ, (609) 859-3333.

Crops:	Blueberries.
Season, Hours:	Mid-June to mid-August. Call ahead for hours.
Directions:	Intersection of Old Indian Mills Road and Route 206.

□ **Giberson's Farm**
New Road, Vincentown, NJ, (609) 859-3634.

Crops:	Blueberries.
Season, Hours:	Mid-June to mid-August. Call ahead for hours.
Directions:	On New Road just off Route 70 east.

□ **Johnson's Corner**
Church and Hartford roads, Medford, NJ, (609) 654-5894.

Crops:	Peas, strawberries, tomatoes, peaches, broccoli, cauliflower, pumpkins, gourds.
Season, Hours:	Mid-May through October. Call ahead for hours.
Directions:	Call ahead.

□ **Lee Brothers Farm**
Route 563, Chatsworth, NJ, (609) 726-9292.

Crops:	Blueberries.
Season, Hours:	Mid-June to mid-August. Call ahead for hours.
Directions:	On Route 563, 4 miles south of Chatsworth.

□ **North Branch Blueberry Farm**
Route 70, Browns Mills, NJ, (609) 893-5693.

Crops:	Blueberries.
Season, Hours:	Mid-June to mid-August. Call ahead for hours.
Directions:	On Route 70 at Mile Marker 30.8.

Mr. McGregor's Garden
Route 537, Jobstown, NJ, (609) 723-1200.

Crops:	Strawberries, raspberries, cutting flowers, lima and green beans.
Season, Hours:	Mid-May through September. Call ahead for hours.
Directions:	On Route 537, .5 mile east of Route 68.

Camden County

Campbell Museum

Campbell Place (off Route 30), Camden, NJ. (609) 342-6440. Monday through Friday, 9 a.m. to 4:30 p.m. Free.

Kids will get a kick out of imagining what it would be like to have their favorite Campbell's soup dished up in one of the imaginative tureens displayed at this small but exquisite company-supported museum. Its impressive collection includes food service utensils, bowls, and tureens that date from 500 B.C. to the present. These containers run the design gamut from a tin-enameled earthenware tureen in the shape of a hog's head to a ceramic ship that pops its top to store hot broth below decks.

Camden County Historical Society

Park Boulevard and Euclid Avenue, Camden, NJ. (609) 964-3333. Monday through Thursday, 12:30 to 4:30 p.m.; Sunday, 2 to 4:30 p.m. Children, free; adults, $2.

The Camden County Historical Society administers two terrific sites at this location. At Panoma Hall your family can compare its 20th-century lifestyle with the day-to-day existence of the Cooper family, who lived and worked in this house in the 18th and early 19th century. In the society's museum building young visitors will enjoy exhibits that include a one-room schoolhouse, an early fire engine and other fire-fighting equipment, and displays of old glass objects, toys, and lighting devices. Early handicrafts and materials on the history of Camden County and its many ethnic groups are also on view.

The society has a number of special reserved children's programs at the site. Groups of young visitors tour both facilities and then try their hand at open-hearth cooking or spinning. For young students or campers unable to make a group visit, the society offers a "suitcase" program. A society representative travels to the classroom equipped with a film and a suitcase full of artifacts to present one of the two traveling children's presentations currently available, "Colonial Life in Southern New Jersey," or "Camden County during the Victorian Era."

Clementon Amusement Park

144 Berlin Road, Clementon, NJ. (609) 783-0263. Memorial Day through Labor Day: Noon to 10 p.m. $8.75 per person; children under 2, free.

This is an old-fashioned amusement park located on a picturesque lake. While its rides have been updated, it preserves an unusual quaintness for an amusement park of its size. Over 25 different rides are offered for a flat fee, seven of which are geared to little kids and housed in the Kiddieland section. You can circle the park on board a miniature train or enjoy the view from the Clementon Bell, a mock-Mississippi River boat that paddles around the lake. On weekends, clowns, a strolling band, and high diver performances occur several times during the day. The face painter invites kids to be a clown or at least look like one. Water slides are available for an additional charge. The snack bar menu includes a decent selection of grilled foods and cold drinks, and covered and open-air picnic facilities are available.

Greenfield Hall

343 Kings Highway, Haddonfield, NJ. (609) 429-7375. September through May: Tuesday and Thursday, 2 to 4:30 p.m. Free.

This well-appointed Georgian structure features period furnishings and the personal memorabilia of Elizabeth Haddon, a member of the family for whom this quaint town was named. Greenfield Hall's display of antique dolls will enchant young visitors.

Indian King Tavern
233 Kings Highway, Haddonfield, NJ. (609) 429-6792. Wednesday through Friday, 9 a.m. to 5:30 p.m.; Saturday, 10 a.m. to 5:30 p.m.; Sunday, 1 to 5:30 p.m. Free.

During the Revolutionary War, this early tavern, once owned by Dolly Madison's uncle, was a meetingplace for politicians and patriots. Helpful guides enjoy sharing the building's history on a tour that includes the colonial kitchen, dining rooms, and bedroom. Kids will enjoy the tavern's exhibit of period toys.

Camden County "Pick Your Own" Farms

□ Springdale Farm
1638 Springdale Road, Cherry Hill, NJ, (609) 424-1743.

Crops:	Strawberries, green and lima beans, cutting flowers.
Season, Hours:	Mid-May through September, daily, 9 a.m. to 4 p.m.
Directions:	Just off Route 70 east in Cherry Hill.

Cumberland County

Cohanzick Zoo
Mayor Aitken Drive, Bridgeton City Park, Bridgeton, NJ. (609) 455-3230.
Zoo Grounds: Daily, 8 a.m. until dusk. Primate Complex: Daily, 9 a.m. to
4:30 p.m. $1 fee for parking.

Located in the 1,200-acre Bridgeton City Park, the Cohanzick Zoo is the
oldest public zoo in New Jersey. Growing in scale and size since its founding in 1934, the zoo now houses over 200 birds and mammals from
around the world. In the Primate Complex visitors can see white-handed
gibbons, ring-tailed lemurs, and cotton-topped and golden lion tamarins.
Black bears can be observed playing in the pool and waterfall of the zoo's
popular Bear Country Exhibit. Through the zoo's recent expansion more
space has been allotted to create comfortable natural habitats for tigers,
cougars, leopards, zebras, bald eagles, North American songbirds, deer, bison, and wolves. Pony rides are a kid-pleasing activity scheduled at the zoo
on summer weekends. Picnic grounds, food concessions, and restrooms are
available.

Nail House Museum
Mayor Aitken Drive, Bridgeton City Park, Bridgeton, NJ. (609) 455-4055.
April through December: Tuesday through Friday, 10:30 a.m. to 3:30 p.m.;
Sunday, 11 a.m. to 4 p.m. Free.

This 1815 wooden structure, once the office of the Cumberland Nail and
Iron works, houses interesting tools and artifacts from a once thriving iron
and nail cutting industry that was powered by the waters of the nearby

Cohanzick River. Featured are the old nail master's desk, an early water cooler, and nail and spike cutting equipment. Also displayed is a two-faced clock. The face that appears in the building interior kept time for the master. Men working outside on the premises checked the hour on the other face of the same clock, visible from the building's exterior. When mass-produced nails made the hand-cutting process obsolete at the turn of the century, glass was the product produced. Glass artifacts from that period are also displayed.

New Sweden Farmstead Museum
Mayor Aitken Drive, Bridgeton City Park, Bridgeton, NJ. (609) 451-4802. March through December: Tuesday through Sunday, 10 a.m. to 3 p.m. Children, $1; adults, $2.

To commemorate the 350th anniversary of permanent European settlement in the Delaware Valley, the New Sweden Company built and opened this replica 17th-century Swedish farmstead in 1988. Guides are usually available to describe what might have gone on in each of the seven log structures that make up the farm. They include the blacksmith shop, storehouse, threshing barn, stable, residence, barn, and firehouse. Costumed interpreters conduct demonstrations of early Swedish colonial crafts at specified times. Call ahead for details on the crafts demonstrations schedule.

Wheaton Village
Tenth and G streets, Millville, NJ. (609) 825-6800. April through December: Daily, 10 a.m. to 5 p.m. Children, $2; adults, $4.

Wheaton Village is an 88-acre Victorian enclave dedicated to the glass industry that still thrives today in Cumberland County. In the Museum of Glass, a stately turn-of-the-century structure, the history of glass is traced through glass objects that range in age from prehistoric to contemporary. Cut glass decorative items along with doorknobs, medicine bottles, paperweights, and chandelier prisms are displayed. Kids will enjoy the demonstration at the Glass Factory gallery where visitors watch the gaffers shape molten glass, heated in a blast furnace, into a variety of utilitarian and decorative items. Printers, potters, weavers, spinners, and tinsmiths demonstrate their craft skills in the shops of the 1880 Crafts and Trades Row. A Victorian School House and Train Station are another part of the tour that appeals to kids. A ride on Wheaton's miniature train is included in the flat admission price. At the General Store kids can buy penny candy from old-fashioned glass jars. The Pharmacy features an old-fashioned ice cream parlor.

There is a restaurant on the premises, but visitors are also welcome to pack a lunch and picnic in designated areas.

Cumberland County "Pick Your Own" Farms

□ Gasper P. Sparacio Farms
Parvins Mill Road, Rosenhayn, NJ, (609) 451-4859.

Crops:	Peas, strawberries, tomatoes.
Season, Hours:	Call ahead for crop reports and hours.
Directions:	Just off Route 56.

□ Genoa Farms
5449 Genoa Avenue, Vineland, NJ, (609) 794-2065.

Crops:	Peas, strawberries.
Season, Hours:	Call ahead for crop reports and hours.
Directions:	Just off Route 540.

□ Nate Bisconte Farm
Morton Avenue and Lebanon Road, Rosenhayn, NJ, (609) 455-3405.

Crops:	Strawberries.
Season, Hours:	Mid-May to mid-June. Call ahead for hours.
Directions:	Off Route 56.

Gloucester County

Red Bank Battlefield
National Park, NJ. (609) 853-5120. Daily, dawn to dusk. Free.

It was here that Revolutionary War General Christopher Greene, hand picked by George Washington, outwitted the Hessian brigades in the defense of Fort Mercer, built on the banks of the Delaware River as a downstream defense against British ships transporting arms and supplies to Philadelphia. Monuments, cannon, and trenches that were part of the earthenworks fort are preserved by the park, which was once administered by the federal government and is now part of the county park system.

On the grounds of the park, the story of the Revolution is told from the perspective of a local Quaker family in their early stone and brick farmhouse, built in 1748. Named for its mistress, the Ann Whitall House served as a temporary hospital for soldiers wounded in the battle. The house, currently opened for guided tours on summer weekends from 1 to 4 p.m., is an ongoing restoration project. When renovations are complete, open hours will be extended and children's reserved group programs will be scheduled.

While visiting the park, take advantage of its riverside walkways, piers, open-air and covered picnic facilities, and playground.

Gloucester County "Pick Your Own" Farms

☐ **Cedarvale Farms**
Repaupo Road, Swedesboro, NJ, (609) 467-2832.

Crops:	Strawberries.
Season, Hours:	Mid-May to mid-June. Call ahead for hours.
Directions:	Take Exit 14 off Route 295. Travel 1 mile west.

□ **Fruitwood Orchards**
Route 538, Hardingville, NJ, (609) 881-7748.

Crops:	Apples, peaches, sour cherries, raspberries.
Season, Hours:	May through September. Call ahead for hours.
Directions:	Route 538 between Mile Posts 9 and 10.

□ **Mood's Farm**
Route 77, Mullica Hill, NJ, (609) 478-2500.

Crops:	Apples, blackberries, blueberries, cherries, grapes, nectarines, pears, plums, raspberries, green beans.
Season, Hours:	Mid-May through October. Call ahead for hours.
Directions:	Six miles south of Mullica Hills on Route 77.

□ **Pantane's Farm**
100 Democrat Road, Gibbstown, NJ, (609) 423-2726.

Crops:	Cantaloupes, cucumbers, eggplants, squash, tomatoes, turnip greens, peppers, watermelons.
Season, Hours:	Late June through September. Call ahead for hours.
Directions:	Take Exit 16-B off Route 295.

□ **Tuck-A-Lou Farms**
Hardingville, NJ, (609) 881-0393.

Crops:	Strawberries, peaches, apples, blueberries, peas, blackberries, raspberries.
Season, Hours:	Mid-May through October. Call ahead for hours.
Directions:	Intersection of Routes 538 and 619.

☐ **U-Pick Farm**
Mullica Hill, NJ, (609) 478-2864.

Crops:	Peaches, apples, green beans, okra, black-eyed peas, eggplants.
Season, Hours:	Mid-June through October. Open daily; call for hours.
Directions:	Intersection of Routes 45 and 538.

Mercer County

Princeton

Drumthwacket (New Jersey Governor's Residence)
354 Stockton Street, Princeton, NJ. (609) 924-3044. Tuesday, noon to 2 p.m. or by appointment. Free.

As Dorothy said in *The Wizard of Oz*, "There's no place like home." New Jersey's CEO would surely agree. Drumthwacket, the official governor's residence since 1983, is not only a house steeped in history, but a good place for a family visit. It was built in 1835 by New Jersey's 28th governor, Charles Olden, who built it on land that had been in his family since 1696. The original Olden farmhouse still stands on the property. In 1893 it was purchased by Moses Pyne, a Princeton University trustee, treasurer, and patron of the arts, who added a Gothic library and the formal terraced gardens that are now being restored. On display in the house are paintings by Charles Wilson Peale and his son, Rembrandt; the table silver from the *U.S.S. New Jersey* and the governor's china dinner service. A visit to Drumthwacket gives the family a feel for the pomp and ceremony of high public office.

Princeton Battlefield State Park and Clarke House
Mercer Street, Princeton, NJ. (609) 921-0074. Park: Daily, dawn to dusk; free. House: Wednesday through Friday, 9 a.m. to 5 p.m.; Saturday, 10 a.m. to 5 p.m.; Sunday, 1 to 5 p.m; free.

Here you can trace the Revolutionary War battle that took place in January 1777, shortly after Washington's troops made their famous crossing on Christmas Day. The ancient Mercer Oak, a giant tree that still stands in the park, is a living memorial to the patriotic general who was slain by the British at this site. Other points of interest in the park are a war monument, a ceramic tile battle map and a marker that identifies a common grave in which soldiers from both sides were buried. For those not interested in history, the park has nature trails for hiking in any season. These trails attract many cross-country skiers to the park during the winter. Picnic facilities are also available.

While visiting the park, plan to tour the Thomas Clarke House. Built in 1770 by a Quaker farmer, the house has been restored to reflect the tastes and lifestyle of its original owner. Restoration and re-creations of the original farm's fields, gardens, and outbuildings are currently underway. Guides, who take a "living history" approach to the house, share home-spun details of life on an 18th-century Quaker farm. They are interested and responsive to visitors of all ages.

Special reserved children's programs are designed to meet the needs of specific age groups. At the site, children's groups tour the battlefield and house and participate in 18th-century games and outdoor cooking demonstrations. In addition, Clarke House volunteers will travel to a school or camp to present a program on various aspects of 18th-century life.

Princeton University Art Museum

McCormick Hall, Princeton University Campus, Princeton, NJ. (609) 452-3787. Tuesday through Friday, 10 a.m. to 4 p.m.; Saturday, 10 a.m. to 5 p.m.; Sunday, 1 to 5 p.m. Free.

This museum is a treasure trove of objects, yet it is manageable and not intimidating for young visitors. There are exhibits of ancient Roman and Greek antiquities discovered on digs sponsored by the University Archeology Department. Pre-Columbian and medieval works are also on view. The Far East collection includes Chinese scroll paintings, bronzes, and Japanese ink drawings. A stained-glass window from famed Chartres Cathedral is exhibited along with the work of Italian Renaissance painters and sculptors. American artists, colonial to contemporary, are well represented in exhibits of painting, drawing, prints, sculpture, furniture, and decorative arts.

The museum offers special nonreserved half-hour programs for children each Saturday morning at 11 a.m. during the September-to-May academic year. A faculty member, student, or docent introduces young visitors to an aspect of art that relates to the collection. Many of the programs include a hands-on demonstration in a fine-arts medium such as pottery, drawing, painting, photography, or calligraphy.

Princeton University Natural History Museum

Guyot Hall, Princeton University Campus, Washington Road, Princeton, NJ. (609) 452-3000. Monday through Friday, 9 a.m. to 5 p.m. Free.

Dinosaur fossils, exhibits on ancient man, and a wide range of displays on fish and birds will delight young visitors to this university museum. The oldsters who accompany them will find the museum's collection of Audubon etching plates particularly interesting.

Trenton

Meredith Havens Fire Museum

244 Perry Street, Trenton, NJ. (609) 989-4039. Daily, 10 a.m. to 8 p.m. Free.

This specialized museum features antique fire-fighting equipment and Civil War memorabilia from the Sons of Union Veterans' collection. If firemen and their equipment are exciting to your kids, they'll enjoy seeing how the job was done in the old days.

New Jersey State Museum

205 West State Street, Trenton, NJ. (609) 292-6308. Tuesday through Saturday, 9 a.m. to 4:45 p.m.; Sunday, 1 to 5 p.m. Free.

This general museum has something for everyone. Adults will enjoy the exhibit of New Jersey decorative arts that includes furniture, ceramics, silver, and needlework crafted in the Garden State. Paintings, drawings, sculpture, prints, and photographs by early and contemporary American artists are also on view. The dinosaurs, mastodons, ecological dioramas, and make-believe mine in the Hall of Natural Sciences are sure to attract the kids' attention. The museum's collection of New Jersey Indian tools, arrowheads, axes, and clothing is also inviting. For stargazers, the astronomy exhibits and weekend planetarium shows fill the bill. There is also an impressive collection of stuffed North American mammals presented in lifelike settings. Changing exhibitions are scheduled throughout the year. There are two museum shops, one that caters to adults and one that carries toys, books, games, and doodads that appeal to children.

Reserved group tours and programs for children are available. Together the museum staff and classroom teacher plan group visits based on the age of the students and the subjects they are studying.

Old Barracks Museum
Barracks Street, Trenton, NJ. (609) 396-1776. Monday through Saturday, 10 a.m. to 5 p.m.; Sunday, 1 to 5 p.m. Children 12 and under, 50¢; adults, $2.

Originally constructed to house British soldiers during the French and Indian Wars, the Old Barracks were built in 1758 to relieve local citizens from the responsibility of housing and feeding soldiers who were stationed in New Jersey during the winter months after returning from various campaigns on the frontier. It was here that the occupying Hessian soldiers, sleeping off their yuletide revelry, were surprised by an attack led by George Washington, who had crossed the Delaware with his troops on a cold and miserable Christmas Day.

Knowledgeable costumed guides accompany visitors on the tour, which includes a recreated barracks room with a three-level bunk bed, the more genteel quarters of an officer, period rooms that feature 18th- and early 19th-century domestic furnishings and decorative arts, and a series of nine sound-and-light dioramas that depict the history of the battles of Trenton and Princeton.

Special children's programs and activities include a reserved summer day camp that acquaints campers with the home and work life of Revolutionary War Soldiers, a museum slide show available to children's groups, and *Spirit of 1776,* a children's play presented at the school that reveals the life and times of a Revolutionary War soldier and his family.

Trenton City Museum
Cadwalader Park, Parkside Avenue, Trenton, NJ. (609) 989-3632. Tuesday through Saturday, 11 a.m. to 3 p.m.; Sunday, 2 to 4 p.m. Free.

Housed in a restored Victorian Mansion called Ellarslie, this city museum, located in a park, features changing exhibitions of local artists' works along with a permanent collection of artifacts and materials that relate to early local history.

William Trent House

15 Market Street, Trenton, NJ. (609) 989-3027. Monday through Friday, 10 a.m. to 4 p.m.; Sunday, 1 to 4 p.m. Children, 25¢; adults, 50¢.

How did Trenton get its name? From William Trent, the man who built this stately dwelling in 1719. The house was later occupied by Dr. William Bryant, a Tory physician who put politics aside and treated injured soldiers from both sides during the Revolutionary War Battle of Trenton. American Col. James Cox later purchased the house, where he entertained such guests as Washington and Lafayette. Until 1954, the house served as the official governor's residence. It has since been restored to the colonial period and houses an exceptional collection of period furnishings. The informative guides are happy to share the history of the house with visitors of all ages.

Suburban Princeton/Trenton

Hopewell Museum

28 East Broad Street, Hopewell, NJ. (609) 466-0103. Monday, Wednesday, Saturday, 2 to 5 p.m. Free.

This small community museum is an entertaining and educational place to spend an hour or two with the kiddos. Its various collections include 18th- and 19th-century furniture, china, silver, pewter, tools and farm implements, and costumes including an old lace wedding gown and a dress worn to President Lincoln's Inaugural Ball in 1865. Of special interest to children is the museum's collection of Indian artifacts and handicrafts.

Howell Living History Farm

Hunter Road, Titusville, NJ. (609) 397-0449 or 737-3299. Tuesday through Saturday, 10 a.m. to 4 p.m.; Sunday, noon to 4 p.m. Closed every Monday and throughout the month of August. Free.

On this turn-of-the-century farm, families see what agrarian life was like almost a hundred years ago. Farmers use early equipment to plant and harvest crops. Eggs are gathered in the hen house. Livestock is fed and cared for. Fruits and vegetables are picked and preserved. Ice from the stream is cut and stored in insulating layers of sawdust and straw to later fuel the family icebox. Sheep are raised for slaughter, and wool is spun and sold to visitors.

Howell Farm interpreters don't deliver pat spiels. Learning takes place on a one-to-one basis as visitors accompany the staff at their daily tasks. Hands-on participation is the rule rather than the exception. Although a family visit is worthwhile any day, special farming activities are always scheduled on Saturdays.

Children's reserved group programs are also available. Program activities are planned by the farm staff based on the season of the year and age of the group.

Washington Crossing State Park

Routes 29 and 546, Titusville, NJ. (609) 737-2515. Park: 8 a.m. to dusk. Parking fee Memorial Day through Labor Day. Visitor Center: Memorial Day through Labor Day, daily, 9 a.m. to 5 p.m.; Labor Day through Memorial Day, Wednesday through Saturday, 9 a.m. to 5 p.m.; free. Ferry House: Wednesday through Saturday, 9 a.m. to 4 p.m.; Sunday, 1 to 4 p.m.; free. Nelson House: Memorial Day through Labor Day, Thursday through Saturday, 11 a.m. to 5 p.m.; Sunday, 2 to 5 p.m.; free.

This is where George Washington and company landed after a nine-hour effort to cross the perilous, snow-swept Delaware River on Christmas Day 1776. A tour of this 807-acre park begins at the visitor center, where the story of the crossing is told in a series of audiovisual exhibits and displays such as an excellent collection of Revolutionary War memorabilia including uniforms and muskets. Two historic properties on the park grounds along the river are open to the public. In the Ferry House, the work and family life of an 18th-century ferry boat master and farmer is interpreted for visitors by costumed guides. At Nelson House, open only during the summer months, visitors view a permanent flag exhibit, changing displays of early American crafts, and a replica of the boat that brought Washington across the river.

Mercer County "Pick Your Own" Farms

□ Grover Farm

348 Village Road, Princeton Junction, NJ, (609) 799-1195.

Crops:	Peas, potatoes, strawberries, pumpkins, sweet corn, asparagus.
Season, Hours:	Late April through October. Call ahead for hours.
Directions:	Near Dutch Neck east of Route 1 via Route 571.

□ Terhune Orchards

330 Cold Soil Road, Princeton, NJ, (609) 924-2310.

Crops:	Apples, flowers, peaches, pumpkins, raspberries.
Season, Hours:	Call ahead for crop reports and hours.
Directions:	Off Carter Road, south of Princeton. Look for signs.

Salem County

City of Salem

Many people see the quaint town of Salem only from their cars as they stop at traffic lights on the well-traveled road to the beaches of southern New Jersey. They don't know what they're missing. It is a town rich with culture, architectural gems, and community spirit.

When John Fenwick and his small band of Quakers landed in Salem in 1675, it became the first permanent English-speaking settlement along the Delaware. The founding of Salem, known to local historians as Fenwick's Colony, predates Penn's arrival by a full seven years. Fenwick's group was not the first to inhabit the region, however. He and his followers were preceded by the Lenni-Lenape Indians, the Swedes, the Finns, the Dutch, and a small group of Pilgrims from the New Haven Colony.

It is through its historical buildings that Salem shares its rich heritage with visitors. There are a few sites that are open to the public year round. An outside view of many others, restored and occupied by private citizens, can be enjoyed anytime. Seeing these sites and taking a short walk around town makes for a pleasant family outing. During an April open house, sponsored every other year by the Salem County Historical Society, visitors may tour the interiors and gardens of over 30 historical homes, churches, and municipal buildings not ordinarily accessible. While a little lengthy for bambinos, the open house is an event that would please moms and dads who enjoy history, early architecture, interior design, and decorative arts.

Alexander Grant House

79–83 Market Street, Salem, NJ. (609) 935-5004. Tuesday through Friday, noon to 4 p.m. Children, 25¢; adults, $1.50.

Headquarters for the Historical Society of Salem County, this brick structure was built in 1721 and houses the society's collections of period furnishings, antique dolls, Indian artifacts, and old glass. Helpful staff members are happy to answer questions and share anecdotes about exhibit objects with visitors large and small. Also on the premises are a tiny law office, built in 1736, and a barn with a horse-drawn hearse and a wooden water pump.

Hancock House

Route 49, Salem, NJ. (609) 935-4373. Wednesday through Friday, 9 a.m. to noon and 1 to 6 p.m.; Saturday, 10 a.m. to noon and 1 to 6 p.m.; Sunday, 1 to 6 p.m. Free.

Built of brick in the Flemish bond design, this was the home of Quakers William and Sarah Hancock, whose initials appear on the date stone. Built in 1734, the home was the site of a senseless massacre during the American Revolution. While Salem's Quaker residents wouldn't actively engage in the battle, they did supply humanitarian aid to Washington and his troops in the form of food. Hearing that Salem farmers had provided the colonial army with cattle, a troop of 300 Queen's Rangers murdered a group of 30 unarmed local men who were stationed at the house to guard a nearby bridge. The house, decorated with period furnishings, still bears bloodstains from the incident.

Old Salem County Court House

Market Street and Broadway, Salem, NJ. (609) 935-1415. Monday through Friday, 9 a.m. to noon and 1 to 4 p.m. Free.

Portions of this stately building date to 1735, but it was almost entirely rebuilt in 1817, and drastically remodeled in 1908. A tour includes the 1817 courtroom, still used by county judges; a replica of Fort Elfsborg, built by early Swedish immigrants; and an exhibit of Indian artifacts on the second floor. Notice the bell on display in the courtroom. It once hung in the courthouse cupola.

Beyond the Salem City Limits

Cowtown Rodeo

U.S. 40, Woodstown, NJ. (609) 796-3207 or 796-3200. Late May to mid-September: Saturday, 7:30 p.m. Children 12 and under, $3; adults, $6.

This ain't the Rio Grande, but it's as close as you'll get in the Delaware Valley, pardner. Cowtown, the longest running weekly rodeo in the United States, is a fun-filled show for old-timers and greenhorns alike. Run by the Harris family for over 30 years, the weekly show includes events such as bareback riding, calf roping, steer wrestling, bull riding, and barrel racing. Cowpokes from Texas, Wyoming, and Oklahoma compete with East Coast contestants for cash prizes. The bucking broncs you'll see performing in the ring have been raised by the family. A well-stocked snack bar and restroom facilities are available.

Fort Mott State Park

R.D. 3, Salem, NJ. (609) 935-3218. June to August: Daily, 8 a.m. to 7:30 p.m. September through May: Daily, 8 a.m. to 4:30 p.m. Free.

One of the prettiest public places along the Delaware, Fort Mott State Park encompasses 104 acres and contains the well-preserved remains of a military installation built from 1896 to 1897 as a seaward defense just before the Spanish American War. It was named for Major Gen. Gersham Mott, a decorated Civil War veteran and native of New Jersey. The property was originally acquired by the U.S. Government in 1838 as part of a master plan to fortify the mouth of the Delaware River. During the Civil War, 2,436 Confederate soldiers who had died while imprisoned at nearby Fort Delaware were buried on the grounds along with 300 fallen Union soldiers.

Visitors tour the fort's batteries, munitions magazine, headquarters, and ordnance buildings on their own. On a clear day, you can see the entrance to the Chesapeake and Delaware Canal and Fort Delaware from the park's scenic riverside lookout. Although there are no guides, the helpful park ranger and his staff are happy to answer any questions. Covered and open-air picnic facilities, playground equipment, and restrooms are available. Fishing is permitted in the fort's moat and off the river beach.

Second Sun Energy Information Center
Delaware River at Lower Alloways Creek, NJ. (609) 935-2660. Tuesday through Saturday, 9 a.m. to 4 p.m. Free.

Public Service Electric and Gas Company has come up with a clever way to educate people about energy and how they generate it. The Second Sun, a refurbished ferry boat moored on the Delaware River near their Salem and Hope Creek Nuclear Generating Stations, is a floating energy sciences classroom. A multimedia show, narrated by William Shatner, traces the history of energy with an emphasis on 20th-century nuclear power, plant design, radiation, and nuclear waste disposal. The interactive exhibits and models housed in the exhibit hall happily engage visitors while they learn about the process of nuclear fission and the related environmental issues its use raises. At Powerplay, Second Sun's video game arcade, the visitor's newfound energy acumen is tested in a series of games that begins with basic energy concepts and ends with complex questions on the generation of electricity and nuclear power.

Second Sun's special services include electricity and nuclear energy demonstrations for kids in grades 4 to 9, reserved plant tours for older students, and half- and full-day teachers' workshops on teaching nuclear and other energy concepts.

Salem County "Pick Your Own" Farms

☐ Bradway's Farm
Jerico Road, R.D. 2, Salem, NJ, (609) 935-5698.

Crops:	Peas, green beans, strawberries, tomatoes.
Season, Hours:	Call ahead for crop reports and hours.
Directions:	Off Route 49.

☐ Daniel Sauder Farm
Almond Road, Norma, NJ, (609) 692-9424.

Crops:	Peas.
Season, Hours:	Call ahead for crop reports and hours.
Directions:	Route 540.

□ Larchmont Farms
Route 77, Shirley, NJ, (609) 358-0700 or 358-3454.

Crops:	Pie and sour cherries, apples.
Season, Hours:	Call ahead for crop reports and hours.
Directions:	Three miles south of Route 40 circle.

Delaware Valley
Calendar of Events

January

Battle Reenactment, Princeton Battlefield State Park, Princeton, NJ
Benjamin Franklin's Birthday, Franklin Court, Independence National
  Historical Park, Philadelphia, PA
Ben's Birthday Bash, Franklin Institute, Philadelphia, PA
Winter Walks, Hagley Museum, Wilmington, DE
Mummers Parade, Philadelphia, PA

February

Black History Month, Afro-American Historical and Cultural Museum,
  Philadelphia, PA
Welcome Spring Exhibit, Longwood Gardens, Kennett Square, PA
Washington's Birthday Celebration, Brandywine Battlefield State Park,
  Chadds Ford, PA
Washington's Birthday Celebration, Washington Crossing State Park, Ti-
  tusville, NJ
Washington's Birthday Celebration, Valley Forge National Park, Valley
  Forge, PA

March

Charter Day, Pennsbury Manor, Morrisville, PA
Maple Sugar Festival, Hibernia Park, Wagontown, PA
St. Patrick's Day Parade, Philadelphia, PA
St. Patrick's Day Parade, Wilmington, DE

April

Craft Fair, Brandywine River Museum, Chadds Ford, PA
Dogwood Blossom Specials, Wilmington & Western Railroad, Wilming-
    ton, DE
18th-Century Market Day, Old Barracks Museum, Trenton, NJ
Farmer's Spring, Delaware Agricultural Museum, Dover, DE
Irish Workers Festival, Hagley Museum, Wilmington, DE
Odessa Spring, Historic Houses of Odessa, Odessa, DE
Salem Open House, Historical Society of Salem County, Salem, NJ
Sheep Shearing, Quarry Valley Farm, Lahaska, PA
Spring Children's Week, Delaware Museum of Natural History, Wilming-
    ton, DE
St. Walpurgis Night Festival, American Swedish Historical Museum,
    Philadelphia, PA

May

Armed Forces Weekend, Penn's Landing, Philadelphia, PA
Craft Show, Colonial Pennsylvania Plantation, Media, PA
Folk Fest, Mercer Museum Grounds, Doylestown, PA
French Alliance Day Celebration, Valley Forge National Park, Valley
    Forge, PA
Israel's Independence Day, Independence National Historical Park, Phila-
    delphia, PA
Old Dover Days, The Green, Dover, DE
Point-to-Point Races, Winterthur Museum and Gardens, Winterthur, DE
Revolutionary War encampment, Brandywine Battlefield State Park,
    Chadds Ford, PA
Wildflower Plant Sale, Ashland Nature Center, Hockessin, DE
Victorian Garden Party, Rockwood, Wilmington, DE

Memorial Day Weekend Specials, Wilmington & Western Railroad, Wilmington, DE

June

Arts and Crafts Exhibition and Sale, Smithville Mansion, Mount Holly, NJ
Colonial Fair, Old Swedes' Church, Philadelphia, PA
Continental Army "March Out," Valley Forge National Park, Valley Forge, PA
Crafts Fair, Delaware Art Museum, Wilmington, DE
Decoy and Woodcarvers Show, Batsto Village, Hammonton, NJ
Elfreth's Alley Open House, Philadelphia, PA
Festival of Fountains (through August), Longwood Gardens, Kennett Square, PA
Flag Day Celebration, Betsy Ross House, Philadelphia, PA
Harbor Festival, Penn's Landing, Philadelphia, PA
Midsummer Festival, Morton Homestead, Prospect Park, PA
Polish Day, Fort Delaware, Delaware City, DE
Sheep Shearing Festival and Craft Show, Newlin Mills Park, Glen Mills, PA
String Band Concerts, Mummers Museum, Philadelphia, PA
Victorian Tea and Tour Week, Rockwood, Wilmington, DE

July

Colonial Crafts Day Camp, Peter Wentz Farmstead, Worcester, PA
Folk Dancing Demonstrations, Philadelphia Museum of Art, Philadelphia, PA
Freedom Festival, Independence National Historical Park, Philadelphia, PA
History Day Camp, Old Barracks Museum, Trenton, NJ
Ice Cream Festival, Rockwood, Wilmington, DE
Independence Day Specials, Wilmington & Western Railroad, Wilmington, DE
July Fourth Celebration, Rockford Park, Wilmington, DE
Old-Fashioned Fourth of July, Princeton Battlefield State Park, Princeton, NJ

August

Hopewell Village Establishment Day, Hopewell Furnace National Historic Site, Birdsboro, PA

New Hope Antique Automobile Show, New Hope, PA

Old Fiddlers' Picnic, Hibernia Park, Wagontown, PA

September

Antique Automobile Festival, Franklin Mint Museum, Wawa, PA

Art, Glass, and Bottle Fair, Batsto Village, Hammonton, NJ

Battle Reenactment, Brandywine Battlefield State Park, Chadds Ford, PA

Boat Show, Penn's Landing, Philadelphia, PA

Brandywine Battlefield Muster, Brandywine Battlefield State Park, Chadds Ford, PA

Cut Your Own Firewood Program (through March), Hibernia Park, Wagontown, PA

Craft Fair, Brandywine River Museum, Chadds Ford, PA

Labor Day Specials, Wilmington & Western Railroad, Wilmington, DE

Family Day, Hagley Museum, Wilmington, DE

Fat Tire Bike Race, Hibernia Park, Wagontown, PA

Puerto Rican Day Parade, Philadelphia, PA

October

Autumn Leaf Specials, Wilmington & Western Railroad, Wilmington, DE

Columbus Day Parade, Philadelphia, PA

Country Living Fair, Batsto Village, Hammonton, NJ

Dark in the Park Halloween Celebration, Hibernia Park, Wagontown, PA

18th-Century Field Day, Red Bank Battlefield, National Park, NJ

Fall Harvest Festival, Delaware Agricultural Museum, Dover, DE

Fall Harvest Market, Brandywine River Museum, Chadds Ford, PA

Fire Prevention Week, Fireman's Hall, Philadelphia, PA

Gothic Gables and Fables, Children's Day at Rockwood, Wilmington, DE

Halloween Ghost Train, Wilmington & Western Railroad, Wilmington, DE

Halloween Party, Quarry Valley Farm, Lahaska, PA

Harvest and Crafts Festival, Ashland Nature Center, Hockessin, DE

Harvest Festival, Colonial Pennsylvania Plantation, Media, PA
William Penn's Birthday Party, Pennsbury Manor, Morrisville, PA
Pumpkinland, Hayrides, Linvilla Orchards, Media, PA

November

Battle Reenactment, Old Fort Mifflin, Philadelphia, PA
Chrysanthemum Festival, Longwood Gardens, Kennett Square, PA
Colonial Thanksgiving, Ferry House, Washington Crossing State Park,
    Titusville, NJ
Farm Animal Day, Ashland Nature Center, Hockessin, DE
Thanksgiving Day Parade, Philadelphia, PA
Tinkertoy Time, Franklin Institute, Philadelphia, PA
Textile Craft Fair, Hagley Museum, Wilmington, DE
Yuletide at Winterthur (through December), Winterthur, DE

December

Candlelight Tours, Ferry House, Washington Crossing State Park, Titus-
    ville, NJ
Children's Christmas, Historic Homes of Odessa, Odessa, DE
Christmas Candlelight Tours, Hagley Museum, Wilmington, DE
Christmas display, Longwood Gardens, Kennett Square, PA
Continental Army "March In," Valley Forge National Park, Valley Forge,
    PA
Crossing Reenactment, Washington Crossing State Park, Titusville, NJ
Crossing Reenactment, Historic Washington Crossing Park, Washington
    Crossing, PA
Farmer's Christmas, Delaware Agricultural Museum, Dover, DE
Hessian Occupation Day, Old Barracks Museum, Trenton, NJ
Holly Night, Pennsbury Manor, Morrisville, PA
Kwanzaa Festival, Afro-American Historical and Cultural Museum, Phil-
    adelphia, PA
Lucia Fest, Old Swedes' Church, Philadelphia, PA
Model train, doll, and Yule decor displays, Brandywine River Museum,
    Chadds Ford, PA
Santa Claus Specials, New Hope Steam Railway, New Hope, PA
Santa Claus Specials, Wilmington & Western Railroad, Wilmington, DE

Swedish Christmas Celebration, Morton Homestead, Prospect Park, PA
Victorian Christmas, Rockwood, Wilmington, DE
Wassail Tour, Colonial Pennsylvania Plantation, Media, PA
Winter Children's Week, Delaware Museum of Natural History, Wilmington, DE
Wreath and nativity set display, Linvilla Orchards, Media, PA

Index

Alice Rowan O'Brien, a freelance writer and public relations specialist, owns and operates O'Brien Communications in Wilmington, Delaware.

Photo credits:

Courtesy of Hagley Museum p. vii, 10; Courtesy of Delaware Museum of Natural History p. 2, 8; Courtesy of Historical Society of Delaware p. 6; Courtesy of Wilmington & Western Railroad p. 13; Courtesy of Fort Delaware Society, p. 18; Courtesy of the Delaware Bureau of Museums and Historic Sites p. 22, 28, 31; Courtesy of the Delaware Agricultural Museum p. 24; Courtesy of Dover Heritage Trail p. 26; Courtesy of Longwood Gardens p. 36, 50, 51, cover; Courtesy of Sesame Place p. 38, 41; Courtesy of the New Hope Mule Barge Company p. 44; Courtesy of the Streitwieser Trumpet Museum p. 48, 54; Courtesy of the Brandywine River Museum p. 58, 60; Courtesy of the Franklin Mint Museum p. 61; Courtesy of the Colonial Pennsylvania Plantation p. 64, Courtesy of the Peter Wentz Farmstead p. 70; Courtesy of the National Park Service p. 72, 73, 92, 93; Courtesy of Mummers Museum p. 99; Courtesy of the Academy of Natural Sciences p. 76, 78; Courtesy of the Franklin Institute p. 80, 81, 83; Courtesy of the Philadelphia Museum of Art p. 84; Courtesy of the Philadelphia Zoo p. 85; Courtesy of Cowtown Rodeo p. 102.